T0279718

LGBTQ+
TRAILBLAZERS
— OF —
SAN FRANCISCO

DR. WILLIAM LIPSKY

THE
History
PRESS

Published by The History Press
Charleston, SC
www.historypress.com

Front cover, top left: Roller skaters, San Francisco, circa 1980. *Photograph by Robert Pruzan. Robert Pruzan Papers (1998–36), GLBT Historical Society. Top right*: Women marching with pride at the Gay Freedom Day Parade, San Francisco, 1977. *Photograph by Crawford Barton. Crawford Barton Papers (1993–11), GLBT Historical Society. Center left*: Gilbert Baker. *Photographer unknown. Gilbert Baker Collection (2017–18), GLBT Historical Society. Bottom left*: Two Victorian women, circa 1870s. *Photographer unknown. Author's collection. Bottom right*: Don at the Russian River, Guerneville, California, 1979. *Photographer unknown. Author's collection.*
Back cover: Two pioneers, circa 1860s. *Photographer unknown. Author's collection.*

First published 2023

Manufactured in the United States

ISBN 9781467151863

Library of Congress Control Number: 2022951582

Remembering
Don Price
(1956–2022)
Beloved husband
Devoted partner
Best friend

CONTENTS

Introduction   7

PART I: O PIONEERS
1. Calafia: Queen of California   13
2. The Story of Chamberlain and Chaffee   17
3. Charley Parkhurst: Man's Work   21

PART II: IMPROPER BOHEMIANS
4. Vestvali the Magnificent   31
5. The Lavender Poet and His Sewing Circle   36
6. Wondrous Women in Pants   41
7. Oscar Wilde: Work of Genius   45
8. Hugged by a Boy on the Barbary Coast   51
9. Putting on the Glitz   55

PART III: PUBLIC LIVES, PRIVATE LOVES
10. Gertrude and Alice: Icons of Modernity   65
11. The French Beethoven and La Creatice   69
12. The Fabulous Baker Street Boys   74
13. The Case for Sexual Liberty   81
14. Clarkson Crane: Cruising Between the Wars   86
15. Elsa Gidlow: Poet, Philosopher, Independent Woman   90
16. The Night They Raided Tait's   94

CONTENTS

17. Esther Eng: Pioneering Filmmaker and Feminist   99
18. Jackie Mei Ling and Chinatown's Female Impersonators   103
19. The Black Sheep in the Blue Book   108
20. Madeline Gleason and the Poetry of San Francisco   114

PART IV: MOVERS, SHAKERS, PORNOGRAPHY MAKERS
21. Hal Call: Activist for Progress and Pornography   121
22. Del and Phyl: Pioneers for Lesbian Dignity and
        Human Rights   127
23. The Drag Queen Who Changed San Francisco   132
24. Vacaville 1956: California's First Gay Rights Protest   138
25. Rikki Streicher: Champion of Freedoms and Rights   141
26. Sisters of Bilitis   145
27. The Trials of Charles Christman   148
28. Wakefield Poole: "No More Closets"   152
29. Sylvester: Queen of Disco   155
30. The Mayor of Castro Street   159
31. Randy Shilts: Reporting Gay History   165
32. Bobbi Campbell: AIDS Poster Boy   168
33. Tom Waddell: Gay Olympian   173
34. Gilbert Baker: Forever Let Us Hold Our Banner High   177
35. George Choy: Passionate Activist   179
36. Trevor Hailey: In the Footsteps of History   182
37. Ken Jones: Equality and Inclusion for All   185
38. Felicia Elizondo: Vietnam Veteran, Transgender
        Rights Activist   189

About the Author   192

INTRODUCTION

We have always been here.

Many of the earliest Californians, including the Ohlone of the Bay Area, believed that because nature was perfect, the diversity of sexual and gender expression in their communities was natural and normal. Sexuality was nature's gift, enduring and indelible, a source of spiritual and healing power. The first Europeans to visit California, however, insisted that same-sex intimacy and gender plurality were "bestial and godless." Although efforts to enforce such views led to dire results for almost two centuries, some still chose to be themselves.

The discovery of gold in California in 1848 transformed San Francisco from a tiny village into a multicultural metropolis of some thirty-five thousand people in five years, with thousands more passing through on their way to and from the mining camps; more than 90 percent of the population was male. Old definitions of sinfulness became irrelevant for at least some of them in a place that the *Daily Alta California* wrote was "by not a few looked upon as a Sodom of wickedness."

Among the multitudes of "the wicked" who moved here, lived here and visited here, many were already or later became celebrated in their generation. Felicità Vestvali and Adah Isaacs Menken were famous before they arrived. Charles Warren Stoddard, Oscar Wilde and Alice Toklas, among others, had their fame in the future. Some, including La Loïe Fuller, are remembered as great artists, writers, performers and personalities. Others, esteemed in their day—Eben Plympton, Annie Hindle, Ella Zoyara—have been largely forgotten.

A few were open about their sexuality, although most could not be and were not. Even so, many of them enabled like-minded San Franciscans, whose names history has lost, to understand that they were not alone. All of them, however, famous or forgotten, residents or visitors, contributed to the development of our communities, some merely by being themselves. In any case, we have much more to learn about the past and the individuals who lived here.

Without their own clubs, shops, organizations and institutions, women and men who desired same-sex relationships met one another through social networks, mutual friends, overlapping circles of community, shared interests and even chance encounters. Because they faced social censure or even prison if their behaviors became known publicly, most lived quiet, anonymous lives. They found places public and private to meet each other and used references, symbols—green carnations, red neckties—and signals to identify themselves.

Not until the Darwinians began classifying everybody and the Freudians began analyzing them did anyone begin to consider that people had a sexuality that might be an abiding human characteristic. Certainly, many of the men caught up in the Baker Street scandal of 1918 knew their desires were inborn. Others were not convinced. Same-sex intimacy remained illegal in California for another fifty-eight years, a passion defined first as a perversion, then a mental illness and then a sexual preference before being understood as a sexual orientation.

Even with the increasing discrimination against them that began after the Great War, women who loved women and men who loved men continued to be attracted to San Francisco:

Clarkson Crane, Elsa Gidlow and Madeline Gleason in the 1920s
Li-Kar in the 1930s
Rikki Streicher in the 1940s
Hal Call, Allen Ginsberg, Phyllis Lyon and Del Martin in the 1950s
Hippies in the 1960s
Sylvester, Harvey Milk, Bobbi Campbell, Randy Shilts and Wakefield Poole
    in the 1970s
Felicia Elizondo in the 1980s

During that time, San Franciscans who sought same-sex intimacy, however they defined and understood themselves, found each other, established communities, opened businesses for themselves, discovered shared goals and common objectives, created organizations and began to realize their common cultural and historical heritage. Their struggles and achievements are intrinsically and integrally woven into the fabric of place and people that is San Francisco.

We will always be here.

The people whose stories are remembered here are only some of those who have come before us. Among the many, many others who easily could have been included are:

Jeanne Bonnet (1849–1876), the "Frog Catcher" of San Francisco

Milton Matson (née Luisa Matson, 185?–?), businessman

Lou Harrison (1917–2003), composer, music critic, music theorist, painter

Guy Strait (1920–1987), cofounder of the League for Civil Education (LCE) and publisher of San Francisco's first gay newspapers

Lisa Ben (née Edythe D. Eyde, 1921–2015) author, editor and songwriter who created the first known lesbian publication in the United States

Pat Bond (1925–1990), openly lesbian actor

Thom Gunn (1929–2004), poet, educator

James C. Hormel (1933–2021), philanthropist, activist, diplomat

Harry Britt (1938–2020), minister, political activist and politician

Robert Opel (1939–1979), photographer, art gallery owner, streaker

Leonard Matlovich (1943–1988), veteran, activist

Charles M. "Chuck" Holmes (1945–2000), adult film producer

John Reed Sims (1947–1984), founder of the first openly gay musical group formed in United States history

Carmen Vázquez (1949–2021), writer, activist, cofounder of the Woman's Building

Marlon Riggs, (1957–1994), documentary filmmaker (*Tongues Untied, Color Adjustment, Black Is…Black Ain't*)

Paul Wotman (1951–2000), LGBTQ+ civil rights attorney

Mark Bingham (1970–2001), public relations executive, rugby enthusiast, hero of 9/11

Many of these profiles first appeared in somewhat different or modified form in the *San Francisco Bay Times*. Many thanks and sincere appreciation to Dr. Betty Sullivan and Jennifer Viegas, copublishers and coeditors, for their friendship, encouragement and support over these past years and their steadfast commitment to bringing past lives as well as current events to their devoted readership.

PART I

O PIONEERS

CHAPTER 1

CALAFIA: QUEEN OF CALIFORNIA

O nce upon a time, long, long ago, "very near to the region of the Terrestrial Paradise," there was a legendary island. "One of the wildest in the world," it was protected by "bold and craggy rocks" that were the strongest "that [are] found in the world." A wondrous realm, it was ruled by a queen "more beautiful than all others, and in the very vigor of her womanhood, valiant and courageous, ardent and with a brave heart." Her name was Calafia. The land she ruled was called California.

In those days, no men lived on the island of California. "It was home to a nation of Black amazons," who like their queen "were of powerful bodies and strong and ardent hearts and of great strength." Brave warriors all, "their weapons were golden and so were the harnesses of the wild beasts that they were accustomed to domesticate and ride." They strictly enforced a "women only" policy; men who ventured into their realm were destroyed by griffins trained to kill them.

"The greatest of the long line of queens who ruled over this mythical realm," Calafia desired "to perform nobler actions than had been done by any other ruler before her." One day, she encountered Radiaro, a great Muslim warrior, who told her that in a far distant land, "all the world is moving in an onslaught against the Christians." Now Calafia "did not know what Christians were," but believing only that "with the great strength of herself and of her women" she would be victorious, she joined the expedition.

Calafia and her warriors arrived at their destination just after a fierce struggle that ended in a stalemate. The great queen, announcing that she

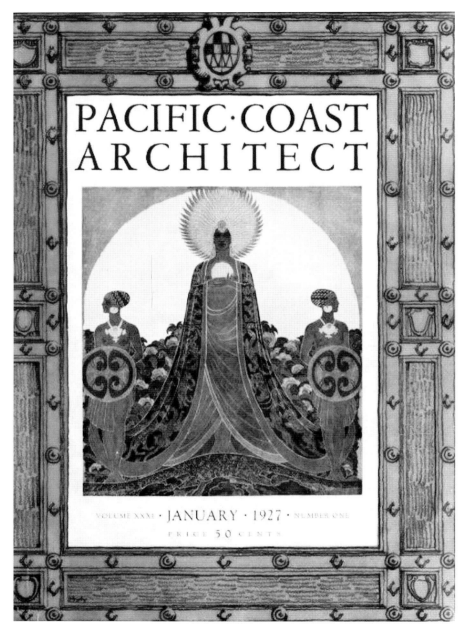

Artists Maynard Dixon and Frank Von Sloun depicted Queen Calafia and two of her warriors in a seven-foot-high panel they created for San Francisco's Mark Hopkins Hotel, 1926. Pacific Coast Architect, *January 1927.*

and her Amazons could do better, took leadership of the Muslim forces. The next day, she "pressed audaciously forward among her enemies" with such skill that "it cannot be told nor believed that any woman has ever shown such prowess." She "dealt with many noble knights, and no one of them left her without giving her many and heavy blows," yet she remained undaunted.

With no victory for either side, the Muslims issued a challenge to the Christians: let them send two warriors to fight Radiaro and Calafia in a single combat to decide the battle. King Amadis, the leader of the Christian forces, and his son Esplandián accepted their proposal. Then the unexpected, the unimaginable, happened.

Calafia, learning from an aide that "Esplandián is the most handsome and elegant man that has ever existed," resolved to see this enemy for herself before meeting him in mortal opposition. Escorted by two thousand of her warriors, she journeyed to the camp of her antagonists. To impress them, she wore a golden toga embroidered with jewels and crowned by a golden hood, raiment fit for a California queen even today. When she finally saw Esplandián, she immediately fell in love with him.

There were hurdles, however, to their romance. First, they had to survive a test of valor on the battlefield. Then there was the matter of an interfaith relationship—to Esplandián, Calafia was an infidel. Even more serious was the fact that they both were physically attracted to women. Additionally, they both held divergent views of females in society: Esplandián believed they were subservient to men in all things; Calafia strongly disagreed. Never mind that he was already engaged to the beautiful Leonorina.

The next day, Calafia dueled with King Amadis and Radiaro with Esplandián. The Christians won. The vanquished surrendered and were imprisoned. During her time in captivity, Calafia—who, after all, did have an eye for women—acknowledged Leonorina's "astonishing beauty" and decided not to compete with her for Esplandián's favor.

Calafia's story had a happy or a tragic ending, depending on your point of view. She converted to Christianity as "the one true faith." She then married Talanque, a handsome knight and valiant warrior, and returned with him to California to establish a new dynasty that would rule over a Christian nation of both women and men.

This tale of Queen Calafia was first told in *Las Sergas de Esplandián* (*The Exploits of Esplandián*) by Garci Rodríguez de Montalvo, published in Seville in 1510 or perhaps earlier. It was the fifth book in a series that told the story

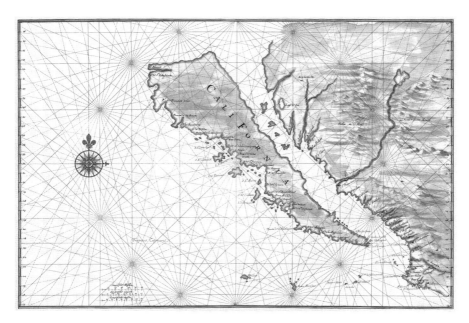

European cartographers, including Johannes Vingboons on his 1650 map, depicted Queen Calafia's realm as an island until the late eighteenth century. *Library of Congress.*

of the conflict between Christians and Muslims during the Crusades. At the time, however, Calafia's land, "rich in pearls," where "there was no metal but gold," existed only in the imaginations of his readers.

The first four volumes of Esplandián's adventures were praised in their day, but this one was pretty much considered summer beach reading when it first appeared. Even so, it was hugely popular and went through edition after edition; according to the author Miguel de Cervantes, Don Quixote had a copy in his library, which his niece and housekeeper later burned for being a bad influence on him.

At least one person among the first Europeans to visit California in the early sixteenth century had read the book. No one knows who that was or who first used the name California for the region, but by 1560, it was appearing on maps and in accounts of travels there. Over time, its source was forgotten, until 1862, when the American author and historian Edward Everett Hale established that it came from Montalvo's novel.

California is unique in many ways but especially in its name. We have states named for a virgin queen, a French monarch, Native American nations, an American president and the wife of an English sovereign, among others. Only California is named for an island realm that was ruled by a Black lesbian.

CHAPTER 2

THE STORY OF CHAMBERLAIN AND CHAFFEE

On January 23, 1849, Jason Chamberlain, a twenty-seven-year-old carpenter, and James Chaffee, twenty-five, a wheelwright, boarded the ship *Capitol* at anchor in Boston Harbor. They had met and become dear friends in Worcester, Massachusetts, in 1846. Now the two bachelors joined some 250 other men—and 2 women, both married—aboard the *Capitol* for a voyage of more than fifteen thousand miles around Cape Horn to San Francisco and the gold fields of the Sierras. They remained in California—and remained a couple—for the next fifty-four years.

Their journey around Cape Horn took 162 days, including stops at Rio de Janeiro and Valparaiso. They arrived on July 20, "in such a dense fog that we cannot see a mile from us," Captain Benjamin S. Buckley wrote in his *Journal of the Voyage from Boston to San Francisco*. There were "hearty cheers" when "that old mud hook went down" into the waters of the bay, Buckley wrote, adding, "May God deliver us from having to make the ocean our home so long again." For many of his passengers, however, their adventure was just beginning.

The Argonauts entered a city of men, "by not a few looked upon as a Sodom of wickedness," according to the *Daily Alta California*. It was a place, one visitor wrote, "lit by the glare of its hells." More than 90 percent of the residents were men. Ladies, usually married, were so few that to see one "walking along the streets of San Francisco was more of a sight than an elephant or giraffe would be today." There were somewhat more women—as opposed to ladies—but they were expensive. Most of the men found companionship with each other.

Chamberlain and Chaffee carried their worldly possessions onto one of the sand hills of Happy Valley, a few hundred feet from the site of today's Palace Hotel, where they pitched their tent. Both quickly found work, earning sixteen dollars a day when that was a week's wages in New England. In a short time, however, the lure of great fortune in the Sierra foothills became too compelling, and they left for the gold fields of Calaveras County.

Their luck was good for a while, but they never did unearth Solomon's mine. Eventually, they settled at Second Garrotte in Tuolumne County. They built a house, meant to last one hundred years (which it did), took up farming, grew vegetables, cultivated apples and manufactured cider and vinegar. In time, they opened a way station for visitors traveling to the Yosemite Valley. Except for those occasions when Chaffee, ever hopeful, went off prospecting, the two men were together every day for the rest of their lives.

Chamberlain and Chaffee embodied the archetype of the forty-niners described by Hubert Howe Bancroft in volume 23 of his *History of California*, published in 1888. "Sacred like the marriage bonds," he wrote of the prospectors, "were the ties which oft united men…yoking them together." These "unions of two," he added, presented "the heroic possibilities of a

Forty-niners Chamberlain and Chaffee, in their cabin they built at Second Garrotte, Groveland, circa 1890. *John Amos Chaffee papers, Bancroft Library, University of California, Berkeley.*

In Chamberlain and Chaffee's later years, their home in Tuolumne County became a way station for tourists on their way to and from Yosemite. *Photograph by A.C. Brown. National Park Service.*

Damon or Patroclus." Few of his readers, educated in the classics, would have missed his allusion to two of the ancient world's most famous same-sex couples.

Friends and neighbors considered them a couple in every regard. Theirs was the only double biography in the *History of Tuolumne County*, published in 1882, which described them as "an example of life-long friendship between men, that is as interesting as it is rare." Since their arrival in California, the author explained, "they have never since been separated." Twenty years later, the *Illustrated History of Tuolumne County* (1901) pronounced them "bosom companions and partners." They were "the first citizens of Second Garrotte."

Were they intimate in all ways? Some of their guests thought so. "The artistic inclination of these gentlemen," one wrote in their guestbook, using a code term for men who were sexually attracted to other men, "is quite apparent, though which one is the 'ladies man' we could not discover, each modestly declining the honor." Another commented on "the wedded bachelors" and a third on their "attachment to each other," which "has the true 'Damon and Pythias' ring." To a third, they were "men after my own Heart."

Given the spirit of the age and its reticence to discuss all things sexual, determining after more than a century who were couples in every sense is difficult. Even those who sought same-sex unions did not necessarily have them with the men they lived with. Whether sexual or not, Chamberlain and Chaffee had a deep and loving relationship.

Chaffee died in July 1903. Chamberlain, by himself for the first time in more than half a century, could not be comforted. "As to being alone," he wrote to an old friend, "there is none that can fill the place left vacant by Chaffee." After six weeks without him, he chose to join his partner in eternity. They had been together, inseparable, for fifty-seven years.

CHAPTER 3

CHARLEY PARKHURST: MAN'S WORK

Everyone knew Charley Parkhurst (1812–1879). For some fifteen years, he was one of the most accomplished, fearless and celebrated stagecoach drivers in California. Described as having a "stout, compact figure, sun browned skin, and beardless face with bluish-gray eyes," he was "the boss of the road" on the routes from Sacramento to Placerville, Oakland to San Jose and San Juan Bautista to Santa Cruz. "Social and generous," he was "never intemperate, immoral or reckless." Not until his death did anybody know that "Cockeyed Charley" had been born female.

The revelation surprised all who learned of it. In Charley's obituary in 1879, the *San Francisco Call* wrote, "The discoveries of the successful concealment for protracted periods of the female sex under the disguise of the masculine are not infrequent," itself a revelation to modern readers. However, the paper, with more than a whiff of disdain, added, "That she should achieve distinction in an occupation above all professions calling for the best physical qualities of nerve, courage, coolness and endurance… seems almost fabulous."

Born in New Hampshire in 1812 as Charlotte Darkey Parkhurst, Charley grew up in an orphanage. At an early age, wrote the *Providence Journal* after his death, "he discovered that boys have a great advantage over girls in the battle of life and he desired to become a boy." With a borrowed suit of boys' clothes, he ran away, "adopted the name Charley, and assumed a masculine presentation." He worked in stables, became an experienced horseman and "soon became an expert whip."

After working as a stagecoach driver on the East Coast for several years, Parkhurst, now in his late thirties, journeyed west, like so many Americans seeking fortune and reinvention in California. He traveled by ship to Panama, traversed the isthmus and then boarded another ship to San Francisco, where he arrived in 1850 or 1851. He took a job with James Birch, whose company operated on the routes between the gold fields north of Sacramento, and quickly earned a reputation as an exceptional coachman.

The writer and artist J. Ross Browne (1821–1875) described his journey with a driver many believe to have been Charley, "who has driven all over the roads in California," in *Harper's New Monthly Magazine* for May 1865. "I had implicit confidence in [him]," he wrote. "The way he handled the reins and peered through the clouds of dust and volumes of darkness, and saw trees and stumps and boulders of rock and horses' ears, when I could scarcely see my own hand before me, was a miracle of stage-driving."

Browne was deeply impressed with Charley. "He has crossed the mountains a thousand times; crossed when the roads were at their worst; by night and by day; in storm and gloom and darkness; through snow and sleet and rain, and burning suns and dust; back and forth; subject to the risks of different teams and different stages; his life balanced on the temper of a horse or the strength of a screw. This is a career worthy the consideration of the heedless world!"

For their journey together, Browne "was the lucky recipient of…the seat of honor, by the side of that exalted dignitary the driver." His questions were endless. "Do many people get killed on this route?" he asked. "Nary a kill that I know of," although "they kill 'em quite lively on the Henness route." Browne was in good hands now, Charley told him. "Our company's very strict; they won't keep drivers, as a gener'l thing, that gets drunk and mashes up stages." Parkhurst never "smashed" a stagecoach.

Parkhurst became as well known for his bravery as for his staging skills. Held up while driving the route between Stockton and Mariposa, he "defiantly told the highwaymen that he would 'break even with them.'" This he did "when stopped on a return trip." Waiting for his opportunity, he "turned his wild mustangs and his wicked revolver loose and brought everything through safe," the *San Francisco Call* remembered in 1880. Wherever he drove, he was "the boss of the road."

Of course, Charley would never have been hired by a stage line as a woman, nor for any of the work he did as a logger and rancher after retiring as a driver. As always, his eminence was widely noted. "He was known as one of the most skillful and powerful of choppers and lumbermen," the *Call*

Journalist J. Ross Browne drew himself riding in the seat of honor next to Charley Parkhurst on a stagecoach in "Washoe Revisited." *Harper's New Monthly Magazine*, May 1865.

continued, and "his services were eagerly sought for, and always commanded the highest wages," often as much as $125 a month, plus room and board.

The state's "crack whip" continued to live as a man for the rest of his life. He even registered to vote in 1867, more than fifty years before women's suffrage was granted by the Nineteenth Amendment: "Parkhurst, Charles, 55, New Hampshire, farmer, Soquel" read his entry in the official ledger. If he voted— no record has yet been found—then he also was the first known anatomically female citizen to cast a ballot in a presidential election in California.

After his truth became widely reported, the *Providence Journal*, among others, was duly impressed by his accomplishments. "The only people who have any occasion to be disturbed by the career of Charley Parkhurst are the

Headlined "Disguised Herself in Man's Clothing to Earn Her Living," Miss Warren's story received almost a full page in the April 17, 1898 issue of the *San Francisco Call*.

gentlemen who have so much to say about 'woman's sphere' and 'the weaker [sex].' It is beyond question that one of the soberest, pleasantest, most expert drivers in this state, and one of the most celebrated of the world-famed California stage drivers, was a woman."

The "cigar-smoking, tobacco-chewing" Charley was hardly the only one identified as female at birth who appeared in public as male. During the gold rush and after, so numerous were the women who sought jobs dressed as men that businesses made it clear, "No young woman in disguise need apply." How many of them were simply looking for work or for financial and personal independence and how many were also trying to express their authentic identity will never be known.

Opportunities for women who wished or had to work were extremely limited. They could support themselves as washerwomen, servants, milliners, seamstresses and, in some cases, factory workers. They also might find employment as teachers or governesses, but very few had enough education to qualify. Clerkships in stores and offices went to men almost exclusively, although many were considered to be effeminate "counter jumpers," then the slang expression for "unmanly men."

Despite the admonition against doing so, determined women in California continued to seek employment dressed as men for many years, including John Warden. Knowing that a female would not be hired for a job at Fowzer's Photograph Gallery on Market Street, where there was an opening for a retoucher, a Miss Warren, reported the *San Francisco Call* in its April 17, 1898 edition, "adopted male attire to win a position for herself."

Warden "worked among men daily for months without any one suspecting her sex," until "the demon drink" ended her career. Asked one evening to the theater by three coworkers, a libation "to refresh the inner man" made her ill. She immediately "resolved that my disguise would have to be dropped." She confessed to her employer the next day, who, surprisingly, allowed her to continue working there as a woman, showing each and all that women could do "men's work."

Unlike John Warden, San Franciscan Mabel Edison, "only 22 years of age" when she was "found out" in 1902, stated, "I always wanted to be a boy. I always wanted to do things like one." It had been an enduring desire. "I can remember my mother telling me that when I was a year and a half old I always wanted to wear my little brother's clothes. The wish has never left me." Her health, she said, "is better when I am in—the other attire."

Orphaned at an early age, she arrived in San Francisco when she was fifteen. As Mabel, she found work as a telephone operator, earning twenty dollars a month. Trying to exist on such a meager salary eventually became too much for her, so she "decided to carry out the plan that often had suggested itself of wearing boy's clothes." First, she trained her voice to be "deep and masculine" and practiced walking like a boy, knowing "that if I changed I would have to have a stride," and then moved to Los Angeles.

Changing her appearance was the easiest part of her transformation. "I got a suit of boy's clothes and took them to my room. Then I went to a hairdresser's and had my hair cut short," in "regulation Johnny style" and "plastered flat on the sides from a military crease through the center." She returned to her room, put on her new clothes and walked out. Finished with her old gender identity, she simply left her dresses there. "I never went back for them," she said.

Now calling herself Herbert Hoffman, she easily found work in a hotel; she "had been around hotels and knew just about what the work of bellhops was," which was "not too heavy" for her. "She was a very bright bell boy," one of her employers said later. "She seemed to know the business thoroughly and was quite smart. She was one of the smartest boys we ever had." He never suspected she was "masquerading," although "she had some ways that were rather effeminate."

After a month in Los Angeles, Herbert returned to San Francisco. "I beat my way up on a freight train on the brake beams," an extremely dangerous way to travel. The day she arrived, she was hired as a bellboy at the California Hotel but soon went to the Langham, where she worked for the next two months as Theodore Hoffman.

She once was asked, "How could you mingle with the other boys as you must have had to do and keep your secret so well?" She replied, "It didn't seem difficult. I drank with them and smoked cigarettes, for they all use tobacco in one form or another." Although the statement seemed to shock her interviewer more than anything else about her, "she didn't blush as she made [it], as she might have been expected to do."

Eventually, she was found out. According to the October 23, 1902 issue of the *San Francisco Chronicle*, someone recognized her while lunching at the Third Street restaurant, where she had worked in female clothes before leaving for Los Angeles. He notified the police, who brought her to the Hall of Justice, where she confessed.

Mabel/Herbert/Theodore was open about her past. Before her time in Los Angeles, she worked in San Francisco as a girl. She was less open about her future. She once was asked, "Will you go back to the other dress when you have a chance?" Her answer: "That remains to be decided." Probably, we will never know whether she or he did or did not.

PART II

IMPROPER BOHEMIANS

CHAPTER 4

VESTVALI THE MAGNIFICENT

Not for nothing was prima donna assoluta and acclaimed actress Felicità Vestvali (1831–1880) known as the Magnificent. Born in Poland, trained for the opera in Italy, she achieved her greatest celebrity playing men—Figaro, Petruchio, Orpheus—including two of the most famous dramatis personae in English literature: Romeo and Hamlet. Critics were divided about her abilities, but the public adored her, filling theaters and halls in Europe and the Americas for performance after performance.

The secret of her success? Contemporaries noted her great talent, her commanding presence, "her statuesque physique and radiant beauty." Those were important, of course, but Rosa von Braunschweig, a longtime friend, wrote in the *Yearbook of Intermediate Sexual Types* (1903) that "it was mostly due to her Uranian nature that she knew how to overcome all obstacles with masculine energy and that her boundless striving allowed her to achieve the goal to which her genius had predestined her."

She was born Anna Marie Stegemann either in Stettin in 1829 or Warsaw in 1831. In childhood, she wanted to be a priest, but eventually, a life in the theater became her singular desire. With her family opposed, she ran away wearing boys' clothes, finding work as a singer with a traveling company. Eventually, she made her way to Leipzig, where she joined the local opera society, appearing in *Norma*, *The Daughter of the Regiment* and as Agathe in *Der Freischütz*.

Regional success was not enough for her. She enrolled in the Paris Conservatory, where she received "thorough voice training" and where "a friend enlightened her about her Uranian inclination." From then on, wrote Braunschweig, "her lively nature craved the joy of love," although she "considered love merely a flower which decorated her life's path."

Further training followed in Italy. In 1853, she debuted at Milan's La Scala as d'Azucena in *Trovatore*, winning "a threefold triumph as woman, as actress and as singer." Vestvali was immediately invited to London, where, the *Musical World* reported, she "created an immense sensation, was vociferously applauded in everything and absolutely pelted with bouquets of all shades and colors, flowers, herbs and shrubs."

From London, she went on to success in Paris, so captivating Emperor Napoleon III that he presented her with a solid silver suit of armor for her performance as Romeo in Bellini's *Romeo and Juliet*. He was not alone. During her two years in the city, "many beautiful women competed for Vestvali's favor and many a husband had reason to be jealous of the beautiful, chivalrous Romeo."

Vestvali was also a particular favorite of President Abraham Lincoln, who attended several of her appearances in Washington, D.C., in early 1864. The *Evening Star* reported that for her opening night performance of *Gamea; or, the Jewish Mother*, a signature role, on January 25, the theater was "overflowingly filled." Vestvali, the paper proclaimed, was "as usual, magnificent and brilliant." Mary Lincoln, deeply moved by the production, persuaded her husband to attend a second presentation of the play on January 28.

The Lincolns returned to the theater the next night for Vestvali's performance as the dual characters of Alessandro Massaroni and the Count de Strozzi in *The Brigand*, a musical drama. Five nights later, the president saw her as Captain Henri de Lagardere in *The Duke's Motto*. When he was assassinated the next year, she canceled her upcoming appearances because of "my own affliction at the loss of one of my esteemed friends."

As imposing as Vestvali was in these roles, she could be just as formidable offstage. On March 23, 1864, while she was waiting for her entrance during the third act of *The Duke's Motto* at the Brooklyn Opera House, two merchants, admitted backstage, approached her in the wings. One of them, "affecting to admire her appearance in men's clothes, laid his hand upon her person." Then, according to the *Daily National Republican*, he "called her a 'bully boy.'"

Vestvali considered his words "an ungentlemanly, if not absolutely vulgar expression." Drawing the sword she was wearing for her role, the indignant diva attacked him, cutting him severely before he fled. Next, she turned on his companion, but unwilling to share the same fate, "he skedaddled." She "then resumed her duties before the footlights." Newspapers everywhere

Felicità Vestvali appeared as the prima donna assoluta she considered herself to be on the cover of *Ballou's Pictorial Drawing-Room Companion* in 1856. *Author's collection.*

reported the incident. Braunschweig believed "an extraordinary talent, such as Vestvali, is justified in giving full reign to her volcanic genius."

Vestvali made her San Francisco debut on September 11, 1865, at Maguire's Opera House as Angelo Romanio in *Romanio! The Beautiful Demon.* The next day, the *Daily Examiner* announced, "A new star has risen," but the *Daily Dramatic Chronicle* was not impressed. Although she "has a fine stage appearance, a splendid speaking voice, and makes up successfully for a very handsome man," the paper wrote, it concluded, "*she won't do....*We fear we cannot prophecy [*sic*] her success."

The critics, however, were ecstatic about her first performance in *Gamea* on September 15. According to the *Daily Alta California*, "Mlle Vestvali achieved the greatest lyric triumph known to California, and proved to an appreciative audience that she had fully earned the title of 'magnificent,' for this is the only word that can fully convey the idea of her acting and singing." The *Daily Examiner* agreed, telling its readers that "a more effective or artistic piece of acting never has been witnessed on the Pacific Coast."

Thomas Maguire, the colorful impresario of the city's Opera House known as the "Napoleon of the Stage," had promised to pay her for one hundred performances across 130 days. When he did not, a war of words began between them, reported by newspapers nationally. Apparently, Maguire wanted to renegotiate their agreement. After Vestvali refused, "he got insolent," according to the version in the *Grass Valley Morning Union*, calling her a "damned fiend under the mask of a woman."

Threats then followed insults. "Take care," he told her, "you have found the right man; you shall not play a single night in San Francisco. I'll prove you have bones in your flesh and I will break every bone in your body before you leave this country." Vestvali promptly had Maguire arrested for threatening to do her bodily injury. Eventually, he promised he would not

Hamlet became one of Vestvali's signature roles, earning her not only accolades in the United States and Europe but also an audience with Queen Victoria. *Photograph by H. Prothmann, Koningsberg. Theater Museum, Vienna.*

harm Vestvali, and the case settled. She then sued him for $30,000 for not fulfilling her contract.

While she was defending her person and her pocketbook, Braunschweig wrote, Vestvali "withdrew full of bitterness to a villa in the magnificent surroundings of San Francisco. In order to recuperate, she studied the part of Hamlet, about which she had been enthusiastic for years" and which became another signature role; in 1868 alone, she played the character twenty times in London, to glowing reviews and outstanding honors, including a private audience with Queen Victoria.

According to Braunschweig, "From this time also dates her friendship with a Miss E.L., a German actress" who became her principal heir. There were other romances as well, including Jessie MacLean, a New York actress. Allowed to use only coded language, the *Daily Alta* told its readers in 1880, the year she died, that "Vestvali took a fancy to her and carried her off to Europe [for] several years of wild adventure." Actually, Braunschweig claimed, "the relationship lasted until her death."

Many of her intimacies endured. During her final illness, she was "nursed by a Miss G," her last love, as well as Miss E.L., "who came to nurse her also." Although Vestvali "never emphasized her Uranian nature," remembered Braunschweig, who also remained a dear friend, she "belonged to those exceptional beings in art as well as in life whose uniqueness can be understood only by those who understand homosexuality."

CHAPTER 5

THE LAVENDER POET AND HIS SEWING CIRCLE

L ooking out from a photograph taken a century and a half ago is a young swell who almost certainly was the first openly gay San Franciscan. He would not have used that term, which then had a different meaning, for himself or understood the concept of sexual orientation, which did not yet exist. He knew who he was, however. As he wrote to Walt Whitman, who appreciated such awareness, "I act as my nature prompts me."

The passing years have been unkind to Charles Warren Stoddard (1843–1909), whose first work was published under the pen name Pip Pepperpod when he was nineteen. Contemporaries like William Dean Howells found his stories "delicate and charming," but now they seem like flowers pressed into a fussy and cluttered Victorian album: fragile, faded, sentimental, easily shattered. Yet for all the purple embroidery in his prose, its lovely homoeroticism remains.

Readers at the time seemed not to notice it in his writing, but friends and associates knew all about Stoddard's sexual interests. Mark Twain, whose secretary he was for a time in London, described him as "such a nice girl." Rudyard Kipling advised him about his autobiographical novel, which described how like-minded men in San Francisco found each other, and encouraged its publication.

Even Ambrose Bierce, who hated everything and everybody—and certainly did not approve of Stoddard's sexuality—warned him to "avoid any appearance of eccentricity" on a trip to London. Stoddard understood what he meant: he risked prison for following his heart there. Only after Stoddard died did Bierce explain that he came to dislike the author because "he was not content with the way that God had sexed him."

"The love that dare not speak its name" could not be discussed in public then, but it could be intimated. When the *San Francisco Chronicle* reported about Stoddard's departure to Hawaii in 1881, it described his emotional farewell to his friends: "'Kiss me, oh kiss me once more before I part from thee forever,' he sighed, and was carried aboard weeping the hysterical tears of esthetic desolation." Newspapers often winked at such "eccentric gentility" with great enthusiasm.

Stoddard himself believed that men loving men "would not answer in America"—not even "in California," he wrote to poet Walt Whitman, "where men are tolerably bold"—but he often ignored his own advice. In San Francisco, he belonged to several informal, overlapping social networks of sexually like-minded men, meeting kindred spirits at parties, through mutual acquaintances, by chance or as he later noted, "under cover of darkness [where] a fellow can do almost anything." Some became lifelong friends.

Songwriter, singer and "confirmed bachelor" Stephen Massett (1820–1898), who gave the first public performance in San Francisco, was one. He and Stoddard had a mutual acquaintance in Bayard Taylor (1825–1878), whose last novel, *Joseph and His Friend*, was dedicated to those "who believe in the truth and tenderness of man's love for man, as of man's love for women." Taylor apparently believed in both. Twice married, he pursued romance with a number of men. Stoddard thought him unhappy. Pulled between two worlds, he wrote, his life "left his heart unsatisfied."

Theodore Dwight (1846–1917) was another of Stoddard's dear friends. He came to San Francisco in 1869, where he worked for the Pacific Union Express Company. He was three years younger than Stoddard, and the two men got to know each other because of Dwight's contributions to the *Overland Monthly*. Dwight returned

Charles Warren Stoddard was in his early twenties when he posed for a carte de viste portrait at the studios of James Chalmers Jr. and Samuel A. Wolfe. *Author's collection.*

Poet, literary critic, travel writer, novelist, lecturer and diplomat Bayard Taylor first visited San Francisco in 1849 to report about the gold rush. *Photograph by Frederick DeBourg Richards, circa 1855.*

When amateur photographer Theodore Dwight took his own picture around 1890, he was living in Boston with his lover, the writer Thomas Russell Sullivan. *Isabella Stewart Gardner Museum, Boston.*

to the East in 1872 and worked for the Bureau of Rolls at the State Department in Washington, D.C., then as archivist of the Adams family papers and finally as librarian of the Boston Public Library.

The two men soon discovered that they had a great deal in common, including a love of writing, theater and autograph collecting and a passion for collecting pictures of nude young men. Unless they were provably art studies, such works were illegal in the United States, but Dwight willingly risked smuggling them through customs. In 1890, he wrote to Stoddard, "The contest is over and I Have Won! The 83 photos are safe in my bureau upstairs.…Only 35 have been impeached—among them some of yours, but there are others truly exquisite."

Perhaps Dwight's greatest coup was in 1892 when, avoiding "confiscation and imprisonment," he safely brought 337 images through customs. More than 100 of them, which he purchased in Munich, were by Wilhelm von Gloeden and Guglielmo Plüschow, famed pioneers of homoerotic photography; the others he found in London. "The photos were never discovered or their place of concealment examined," he wrote to Stoddard. "When you see my spoils you will comprehend my dangers." The men remained friends for forty years.

Stoddard met the actor Eben Plympton (1853–1915) sometime in the early 1870s. They may have been brought together by mutual friend Jenny Spring MacKay, whose incarnation as "Little Mama" introduces the two in Stoddard's autobiographical novel, *For the Pleasure of His Company.* "There, you are to be brothers, and love one another with brotherly love!" she tells them. "My boys must always meet; and they must always let me plot for them." The two men had a passionate affair, "too intense to last," Stoddard wrote later.

Plympton first appeared as an actor in Stockton in 1871. He became a member of John McCullough's California Theatre troupe in San Francisco, then returned East to join the Lester Wallack Company in New York. Described by the *New York Times* as a "handsome, virile leading man," he was Armand Duval to Helena Modjeska's Marguerite Gautier in *Camille* and Romeo to her Juliet, among many roles. In later years, Stoddard often visited him at his estate in Massachusetts, "to which interesting men of various types" were invited.

Stoddard's first book made him famous. It was published in the United States in 1873 as *South-Sea Idyls* and as *Summer Cruising in the South Seas* in Great Britain the next year, and no one seemed to notice the mild homoeroticism found in such sketches as "Chumming with a Savage," "Joe of Lahaina" or the much more open portrayal of affection between men "In a Transport." "They are," wrote William Dean Howells, "the lightest, sweetest, wildest, freshest things that were ever written about the life of that summer ocean."

In 1885, Stoddard became "Instructor of Belle Lettres" at Notre Dame University. He believed himself well qualified. "I am fond of the society

Handsome, virile leading man Eben Plympton worked with many of the greatest actors of his day. He appeared in Stoddard's autobiographical novel, *For the Pleasure of His Company*, as Grattan Field. *Author's collection.*

of young men and lads," he wrote the administration. "I nearly always win their confidence and attract them to a rather unusual degree." He resigned in 1886, then moved in with a former student and his parents, who accepted him simply as their son's friend; the affair lasted two years. From 1889 to 1902, he taught at the newly founded Catholic University in Washington, D.C.

Stoddard returned to San Francisco in April 1903, where he was feted at a "welcome home" party held at the Bohemian Club attended by the ebullient tenor Enrico Caruso and the very closeted author Henry James. The next year, he published *The Island of Tranquil Delights*. It included some of his older stories, with their disguised homoeroticism, but also some new reminiscences, where he now felt he could be "tolerably bold." Relating "the tales of two horses and their boys" and "our harmless life and adventures," he wrote,

> *It may be that this episode is hardly worth remembering at all, yet I cannot forget it nor refrain from recounting it since it once touched me to the quick. It does not matter if in my calmer moments reason cautions me to beware—my head and my heart don't hitch—they never did—and so*

I have written as I have written; and I shall not have written in vain if I, for a few moments only, have afforded interest or pleasure to the careful student of the Unnatural History of Civilization.

Stoddard never came closer to publicly admitting his heart's desire. Wherever he went, he hoped of finding friendship, romance, intimacy and love with like-minded men.

CHAPTER 6
WONDROUS WOMEN IN PANTS

A lthough Deuteronomy 22:5 expressly forbids cross-dressing as an "abomination unto the Lord," San Franciscans have adored transvestite performance since the earliest days of the gold rush. Like many other admonitions ignored by residents then—and since—no one objected to violations of this particular proscription, at least when it came to the theater. Instead, they embraced the cross-dressing performances of Adah Isaacs Menken, Ella Wesner and their peers, in both serious productions and vaudeville turns, finding these not-always-virtuous women "more precious than rubies."

Possibly the earliest male impersonators to appear in San Francisco were the Bateman sisters, who during the 1850s crisscrossed the United States in Shakespeare's *Richard III*, their favorite production, and other plays. Ellen, nine, wearing a pasted-on mustache, played the title role. Kate, eleven, appeared as Richmond. Already seasoned troupers, they first performed in the city at the Metropolitan Theatre on April 10, 1854. Audiences, reported the *Alta California*, were "struck dumb with amazement." They retired as child actors in 1856.

Local audiences found Adah Isaacs Menken (1835–1868) even more sensational. A true bohemian spirit, she wrote poetry, championed Whitman, praised those who defied social conventions and followed her own inner guide. Her first performance in San Francisco was on August 24, 1863, playing the title character in *Mazeppa*, the story of a young Cossack who is banished for adultery by being tied naked to a wild horse. It became her signature role and ultimate "pants part."

Adah Isaacs Menken as Mazeppa, 1866

SARONY,   37 Union Sq. N. Y.

Wearing flesh-colored tights, Adah Isaacs Mencken dazzled audiences in her gender-bending portrayal of a nude man strapped to a horse as the title character in *Mazeppa*, her most famous role. *TCS 19, Harvard Theatre Collection, Houghton Library, Harvard University.*

During the play, her publicity proclaimed, "Miss Menken, stripped by her captors, will ride a fiery steed at furious gallop onto and across the stage and into the distance." Of course, the horse was more docile than demonic, and Menken was not actually naked—she wore flesh-colored tights—but no one cared. She simply mesmerized everyone, even Charles Warren Stoddard, the city's lavender "boy poet." She was, he wrote, "a vision of celestial harmony made manifest in the flesh."

Stoddard never forgot her. In his long article about her for the February 1905 *National Magazine*, he wrote, "I saw her as a boy, and she inspired in me an enthusiasm that found expression in some youthful verses championing her cause.…I knew her story as it was known of men, but it did not appall me: it woke in me the pity that is akin to love. I am glad that it did then; I am glad that the memory of that emotion does even at this late day."

Adah's behavior and her bohemian circle generated endless questions, scandal and gossip about her sexual self. She was married five times, and her "romantic friendships" with women were discreet. "Do you believe in the deepest and tenderest love between women? Do you believe that women often love each other with as much fervor and excitement as they do men?" she wrote to poet Hattie Tyng in 1861. "I have had my passionate attachments among women, which swept like whirlwinds over me…changing and renewing my capabilities for love."

Perhaps her adoration for Hattie was only platonic, but there were others she also adored. After leaving San Francisco, Menken eventually journeyed to Europe, where she met author George Sand. Both favored short hair, cigars and wearing men's clothes when they dined together. Sand, wrote Menken, "so infuses me with the spirit of life that I cannot bear to spend an evening apart from her." She also was romantically linked with playwright Alexandre Dumas père, among others, but many contemporaries believed she and Sand were intimate in every way.

Ella Wesner (1841–1917), the most successful American male impersonator of her generation, began her career as a ballet dancer in the late 1860s. For a time, she was a dresser for Annie Hindle, the first "great serio-comic and impersonator of male characters," from whom she learned the art of male impersonation. She became famous performing "character songs with rapid changes" and playing "swells," including "Captain Cuff," a cigarette-smoking man about town, and Tom Vapid, a drunken dandy who falls asleep in a barber's chair.

Wesner first appeared onstage in San Francisco in August 1871. The *San Francisco Figaro*, calling her "inimitable," praised "her unapproachable portraiture of Male Character." Because the only entrance to the theater was through a saloon, her performances were for men only. One reviewer regretted that "ladies can't go to the Bella Union, they would all fall in love with [her]." At the height of her success, her great talent earned her as much as $200 a week.

Although Wesner never married, after the murder of notorious robber baron Jim Fisk, she eloped to Europe in 1872 with his former mistress, Josie Mansfield, presiding over a louche salon at the Café Americain in Paris; the only interest the newspapers had in their affair was that it caused Wesner to ignore a signed contract. She returned, alone, the next year to resume her career. When she died in 1917, members of the Actors' Fund made sure her wish to be interred dressed as a man was honored.

Of course, Wesner was only one of numerous male impressionists to entertain the public between the end of the Civil War and the start of World War I. According to the *New York Sun*, her mentor Annie Hindle was the "first out-and-out male impersonator New York's stage had ever seen" when she debuted in 1867. An immediate success, she received endless amounts of fan mail, almost all of it from women. Her first appearances in San Francisco were in 1878.

Left: Ella Wesner, always at the cutting edge of men's fashion when she portrayed swells and dandies onstage, became one of the most successful and highly paid vaudevillians of her day. *Author's collection.*

Right: Each of Annie Hindle's three marriages made headlines in the United States. The last two were to women, although those were not recognized by civil authorities. Only the first was unhappy. *Author's collection.*

Six years later, she made national headlines when she married Anna Ryan, "her dresser and faithful companion," a "pretty little brunette of 25," in Grand Rapids, Michigan. Hindle wore a dress suit, Ryan a "traveling costume." Gilbert Sarony, a well-known female impersonator known as "the funniest man in show business," was best man; there was no bridesmaid. "I know all the circumstances," the minister stated. "I believe they love each other and that they will be happy."

Indeed they were. When Ryan died in 1891, Hindle declared that "the best of her life is gone." The next year, however, reported the *San Francisco Chronicle* in a page one story, she became "the lawful husband of Miss Louise Spangehl" in a ceremony performed in Troy, New York. "Miss Hindle has three times been married," the paper explained. "Once she had a husband and twice she has had a wife, once she was a widow, once a widower, and now she is a husband again." Both onstage and off, she lived her life authentically, "as nature intended."

CHAPTER 7

OSCAR WILDE: WORK OF GENIUS

I t's an odd thing," Lord Henry Wotton once remarked, "but anyone who disappears is said to be seen in San Francisco. It must be a delightful city and possess all the attractions of the next world." He certainly knew what he was saying. Oscar Wilde, his creator and alter ego, had visited for two weeks in 1882. San Francisco "is most attractive," he told one reporter after his stay. With "the most lovely surroundings of any city except Naples," he said to another, it "is the city of fine men and beautiful women!" It remained his favorite American metropolis always.

Before his visit, Wilde was famous primarily for being famous, willing to do almost anything to get people talking about him and his "fascinating, poisonous, delightful theories." Although eventually, he paid a huge price for its success, his strategy worked. His extravagance made him a celebrated icon of the British Aesthetic Movement, his manner satirized regularly in humor magazines, his eccentricities given to Reginald Bunthorne, a "Fleshly Poet," in Gilbert and Sullivan's operetta *Patience.*

Wilde's flamboyance raised indelicate questions about him almost from the beginning, although no one could ask them in print directly. Even Gilbert, never known for sexual frankness, described Bunthorne as having "an attachment à la Plato / For a bashful young potato / Or a not too-French French bean" at a time when a classical education taught that Platonic love was between two men—never mind what the British thought of French masculinity.

Oscar Wilde was famous mostly for being famous when he posed for New York photographer Napoleon Sarony shortly after arriving for his American lecture tour in January 1882. *Library of Congress.*

Americans were less familiar with Aestheticism, so Richard D'Oyly Carte, the operetta's producer, approached Wilde to do a series of promotional appearances across North America. He agreed. (In a fascinating historical coincidence, Carte's son Lucas soon began a romance with Alfred Douglas, who later became the great and ruinous love of Wilde's life.) Because of advance publicity, Wilde was greeted everywhere by thunderous crowds.

When Wilde arrived, old American archetypes of the sturdy farmer and the hardy pioneer were giving way to a more urbane "tender ideal" of manliness. Even so, Wilde and the aesthetic values he championed—a love of artistry, beauty, taste and pleasure—challenged gender conventions and seemed to promote "dreaded effeminacy." Once implying weakness of character or softness of purpose, the term was becoming associated with "men who do with men," known derisively as "Miss Nancys" and "Charlotte Annes."

Propriety forbade reporters from discussing Wilde's sexuality, but they used the same words everywhere to communicate that at best he was unmanly and epicene and at worst, "unnatural." The *New York Times* called him a "mama's boy" with "affected effeminacy." The *Newark Daily Advertiser* described his eyebrows as "the sort coveted by women." The *Boston Evening Transcript* asked,

"Is he manne, or woman, or childe? / Either, / and neither! / She looks as much like a manne / As ever shee canne; / He looks more like a woman / Than any feminine human." Readers easily grasped their meaning.

Such clucking followed Wilde across the continent. When he arrived in San Francisco on March 26, 1882, the *Daily Alta California* called him an "effeminate apostle of unhealthy and morbid laziness." The *Chronicle* was equally blunt. In an article titled "Lo! The Esthete," it expressed a concern that people would mistake him for "Charles Warren Stoddard, who he so resembled in manner and sentiment"—but not physical appearance— "come back in disguise to greet them with a poetic and tender embrace." Because San Francisco's "Boy Poet" was widely known as a "Miss Nancy," the paper blatantly told its readers that Wilde was also; mentioning his "tender embrace" only reinforced this view.

The *San Francisco News Letter*, a weekly, also joined the fray, describing "A Reception to Oscar Wilde" in its March 18, 1882 issue. Although it avoided discussing Wilde entirely, it described a typical aficionado, "the bangs-his-hair young man" who "is in the pink of perfection" and receiving eighty dollars per month as an under-clerk in a wholesale grocery. Its coded language left no doubt about his lack of masculine virtues.

> *He wears a claw-hammer coat, with satin lapels, at all evening entertainments, and stands off his celestial wringer of linens with an indignant and aristocratic air. He reads Rossetti and Wilde and Swinburne, and other authors of the aristocratic school; he is seldom seen without a boutonniere, and aims to wear fresh ones daily, and proudly swells with the impression that he is just too too utterly utter in his utterances.*

Wilde's most disparaging critic was Ambrose Bierce, who described him in the March 31, 1882 issue of the *Wasp* as "that sovereign of insufferables" who has "blown crass vapidities through the bowel of his neck, to the capital edification of circumjacent fools and foolesses, fooling with their foolers.... There never was an impostor so hateful, a blockhead so stupid, a crank so variously and offensively daft....He makes me tired."

As editor of the *Wasp*, Bierce could go even further. In addition to everything else, he wrote, Wilde was "missing everywhere his heaven-appointed functions and offices," a clear indictment of his supposed sexual desires. In the same issue, Bierce also ran an editorial cartoon by G.F. Keller that characterized Wilde as a false, fawning "sunflower messiah" riding a jackass into the city, welcomed and worshiped by many of local

Cartoonist G.F. Keller lampooned Wilde and his grand entry into San Francisco in the March 31, 1882 issue of the *Wasp*, edited by Ambrose Bierce. *California State Library, Sacramento, California.*

society's most prominent denizens. What Wilde thought of Bierce and his comments is unknown.

In San Francisco, Wilde lectured about "The English Renaissance," "Art Decoration," "The House Beautiful" and "Irish Poets and Poetry of the Nineteenth Century." He received very mixed reviews. The *Daily Alta California* described his appearance and his delivery but reported nothing about what he had to say; those who did were mostly negative. Regardless, his stay was a huge success.

Wilde departed the city on April 8, never to return, with all his great and enduring works still before him in that incandescent fin de siècle decade of both his triumph and destruction: *The Picture of Dorian Gray*, *Lady Windermere's Fan*, *A Woman of No Importance*, *An Ideal Husband*, *The Importance of Being Earnest*, *De Profundis*, *The Ballad of Reading Gaol*. Ridiculed from coast to coast for his clothes, his androgyny and his ideas, Wilde, however, had the last laugh. He laughed all the way to the bank.

San Franciscans continued to follow Wilde's career. Local newspapers avidly shared the details of his trials for libel and "gross indecency," although they could not print the specific allegations. Admirers quickly disappeared. Kadir Edwards Davis, pastor of a church in Oakland, who billed himself as the "American Oscar Wilde" on the lecture circuit, stopped wearing a sunflower, cut his hair short and now billed himself as the "Versatile Gentleman," which had a different meaning then; his dilemma was reported nationally.

Such disdain was common during the mauve decade. For an interview he gave in 1897, the chef of the Palace Hotel showed a reporter from the *Overland Monthly* the menus for banquets lauding Patti and Bernhardt, among many others. Only one page was without a title. "That was for Oscar Wilde," he explained. "But I have cut out the name!" So well known was Wilde and his trial that the magazine's editor felt no need to explain why the chef would do so.

Others also took the opportunity to express their disapproval. At one performance of *Patience* at the Tivoli Opera House, a group of several hundred University of California students interrupted whenever the actor impersonating Wilde appeared onstage, although the company continued to stage the operetta occasionally for the rest of the decade.

Wilde's death in 1900 was front-page news. So was his shattered reputation. Eight years after he died, the *San Francisco Call and Post* reported sharp criticism of a Berkeley church journal for publishing two of his poems; given "the personality of the author the poems should have been suppressed," it editorialized. As late as 1918, the paper still characterized him as "the insolent, the buoyant, the defiler of the world."

Isaiah Taber photographed Wilde's parade route up Market Street from the Embarcadero to the Palace Hotel in 1885. The cable cars had only recently been added. *Library of Congress*.

In his final days, Wilde may have disagreed with Lord Henry's comment, "There is only one thing in the world worse than being talked about, and that is not being talked about." He set an example for generations to come by taking his own advice: to "live! Live the wonderful life that is in you!" Because, as he observed, "one's real life is so often the life that one does not lead," we are grateful that those of us "to be seen in San Francisco" can follow his lead to be "our fabulous selves."

CHAPTER 8

HUGGED BY A BOY ON THE BARBARY COAST

The *San Francisco Call* was shocked, shocked to discover there were such goings-on. "Hugged by a Boy," read the headline in its August 3, 1894 issue. Certainly nothing newsworthy about that, as mothers everywhere, after sending their sons to school, could verify. This boy, however, was different. Not dressed in overalls or a Fauntleroy suit or a freshly pressed white shirt and trousers, this boy was not in a classroom, but a barroom— and most definitely not dressed as a boy.

The newspaper summed up the story in mocking terms: "A Female Impersonator Robs a Rustic" and "Will Exchange Skirts for Trousers" that were "Adorned with Broad Stripes." It was about to tell the "laughable" story of a man who "fell in love with a female impersonator, who drank beer with him, kissed him and robbed him."

The female impersonator was Bert Larose, "a beardless youth, with a falsetto voice." According to the *Call*, he "made a precarious living by performing as a woman in Barbary Coast theaters and dives." Originally from Ohio, he stood 5' 5⅜" tall and had blue eyes, chestnut hair and a "florid" complexion. In 1894, he was eighteen years old but looked much younger.

The "rustic" was C.E. Bernick (or Berwick), fifty-eight, of Napa County. He was "an old man whose beard of gray has been caressed by the amorous zephyrs of many summers." Visiting the city for a meeting of the Carpenters' Union, he "subsequently…made his way to the Barbary Coast in search of excitement and steam beer." He had $280 [about $7,840 today] in bills "in his inside pocket when he entered Bottle-Meier's theater" at 513 Pacific Street.

Larose, "nicely painted and wearing his skirts, was sitting at a table with a genuine member of the softer sex. The old man leered at them and they leered back. After a time he sat down with them and drank two bottles of beer [at $1 each, now about $28 each]. It soon became apparent that he was smitten with the fictitious charms of the actor."

Bernick asked Larose "in cooing tones to go with him into a box and drink." Larose accepted the invitation, "and while in the box caressed the graybeard and absorbed all the liquid refreshment that he desired." Shortly after midnight, "Bernick was thrown out of the place.…Wandering dazed about the coast, he was arrested and taken to the old City Prison. His pockets were empty."

Although Bernick first "declared that he had been robbed by the policeman who arrested him," the "accused bluecoat…soon learned what had happened to him at the theater." Larose, "vehemently professing innocence, was arrested and charged with grand larceny."

At his trial, Larose's attorney tried to both embarrass and discredit his accuser, asking him questions to detail the intimacy he had shared with a man forty years his junior. "'Now, Mr. Bernick,'" he asked, "'do you mean to tell me that you thought this boy was a woman?' 'I did so,' faltered the aged one, whose cheeks were slowly reddening." Clearly, the "rustic" could not tell the difference between a woman and a man.

Then the questioning turned to expressions of their tender affinity. "'And you took him into a box at Bottle-Meier's theater?' 'I did.' 'And you caressed him there? 'I suppose so.' 'Kissed him?' 'Maybe I did.' 'And hugged him?' 'I guess so.' 'And he hugged you, did he?' 'Well, I should say he did. That's how he got my money.'" Printed by the *Call*, the testimony was a rare public account of sexual intimacy of any kind between two men.

Female impersonator Bert Larose served four years, two months in San Quentin State Prison after being convicted of robbing a tourist on the Barbary Coast. *San Quentin State Prison Records, California State Archives, Sacramento, California.*

When the *San Francisco Chronicle* reported the same story, it was slightly more sedate but much more specific. Describing the theater as one of the Barbary Coast's "amusement resorts of a doubtful character," it casually mentioned that Larose, whom it identified as "a queer young man," had been "sitting on Berwick's [*sic*] lap and fondling him in an affectionate manner" when he "picked his pocket."

Larose was convicted of grand larceny and sentenced to six years in San Quentin. As prisoner 16065, he began his term on September 4, 1894. After serving four years and two months, he was "restored" on November 4, 1898.

Beginning with the gold rush, San Francisco had the reputation as being a dissolute, amoral city of licentious women and prurient men. As early as 1851, when the population was more than 90 percent male, the *Daily Alta California* noted that the Barbary Coast, especially, was a notorious "haunt of the low and the vile of every kind." Twenty years later, during a bitter political campaign, the paper printed a list of the denizens of the Coast, especially those found on the infamous block of Pacific Avenue between Kearney and Montgomery Streets:

> There's Two-fingered Tom and and his 'roity pal;
> There's Slippery Bill, and Ebony Sal;
> There's One-eyed Montrose, and Oily-cheeked Charley;
> There's Sodomy Mike, and Slung-shot O'Farley.

With only 100 policemen in 1871—one officer for every 1,445 inhabitants— San Francisco was a city where these and many other disreputables could thrive.

No one was more offended by the Coast than Benjamin Lloyd, whose *Lights and Shades of San Francisco*, published in 1876, detailed its unsavoriness:

> The petty thief, the house burglar, the tramp, the whore monger, lewd women, cut-throats, murders, all are found here. Dance halls and concert-saloons, where blear-eyed men and faded women drink vile liquor, smoke offensive tobacco, engage in vulgar conduct, sing obscene songs and say and do everything to heap upon themselves more degradation, are numerous.... Licentiousness, debauchery, pollution, loathsome disease, insanity from dissipation, misery, poverty, wealth, profanity, blasphemy, and death are there. And Hell, yawning to receive the putrid mass, is there also.

So it remained until the Great Earthquake and Fire of 1906 destroyed the area and the city finally stepped in to clean it up for the last time in 1913.

Before that happened, however, the *Call* printed another scandalous same-sex story about the Coast in 1908, the year Billy Harrington and two silent partners bought the Seattle Concert Hall at 574 Pacific Street. Harrington renamed it the Dash, installed a row of private, curtained booths on each side of the dance floor and ensconced "male degenerates who wore women's clothing" in them. For a consideration, they entertained customers "in a way that may be imagined, but may not be described."

Unable to detail the specific entertainments they provided, the newspaper could only describe the establishment as "one of the vilest saloons and dance halls ever maintained in San Francisco," the "home of unspeakable vices and the most depraved type of men." It delighted, however, in revealing that Harrington's two silent partners were officers in the courtroom of superior court judge Carrol Cook.

The newspaper had opposed Cook for years, and its revelations led to his defeat in the fall election. The Dash closed soon after. Not until twenty years later, when the Finocchios allowed gay men to have a quiet corner of their speakeasy at Sutter and Stockton Streets, was there a single bar or club in San Francisco where those of a "refined nature" could meet.

CHAPTER 9

PUTTING ON THE GLITZ

She was one of the most handsome performers ever to grace a San Francisco theater. Men honored her. Women emulated her. Elegance, poise, bearing—all were hers. Onstage, she was the fascinating widow, the crinoline girl, cousin Lucy. Offstage she was Julian Eltinge (1881–1941), the most famous and extraordinary cross-dresser in the world.

San Francisco always welcomed female impersonators. At the city's first public performance on June 22, 1849, given in the schoolhouse at the northwest corner of Portsmouth Square, Stephen Massett (circa 1820–1898)—a composer whose popularity then rivaled that of Stephen Foster—gave "a concert of vocal music interspersed with recitations and imitations." Although tickets cost $3 each, the event was a success; after expenses, which included moving a piano from the Customs House for $16, the event earned over $500.

Among Massett's imitations was one of Madame Anna Bishop, a world-famous prima donna assoluta, singing "The Banks of the Guadalquiver." (Many believed the author George du Maurier used Bishop's relationship with Nicolas-Charles Bochsa as the basis for the characters Svengali and Trilby in his 1894 novel *Trilby*.) He also did an impression "of an elderly lady and a German girl, who applied for the situations of soprano and alto singers in one of the churches in Massachusetts." His audience included four women, "probably all there were in town."

Massett apparently never performed in women's clothes, but Omar Kingsley did. Born in St. Louis in 1840, he ran away to the circus when

Until she was revealed to be Omar Kingsley, Ella Zoyara influenced women's fancies for "an Ella hairstyle," "an Ella waistline," "Ella combs," "Ella fans" and "Ella imitation jewellery." *Musée des Civilizations de l'Europe et de la Méditerranée, Marseille.*

he was eight years old. He learned to be a trick rider, touring Europe for years as Ella Zoyara, dazzling audiences everywhere. London was typical. According to Thomas Frost, writing in 1881, "The young artiste's charms of face and form were a never-ending theme of conversation and meditation for the thousands of admirers who nightly followed them round the ring with enraptured eyes."

Royalty was equally captivated. A Russian count offered a large sum of money for an introduction to "Mademoiselle Ella." The King of Sardinia, later Victor Emmanuel II of Italy, presented a medal "to the Illustrious Lady...as a tribute to her equestrian skill and her virtues as a lady." Ever demure, she required a female chaperone for her private audience with him.

On her return to the United States, Zoyara was billed as "the greatest female rider that Europe had ever seen." She first performed in San Francisco in 1863; later, the *San Francisco Chronicle* described her as "more daring and brilliant than any equestrienne that had or has appeared before an American audience." After two years touring the West Coast, she sailed for Australia.

Because Kingsley dressed "in female attire on steamers, on the streets, in hotels, and in the circus," wrote the *Chronicle* after his death in 1879, the surprise of those who saw him one day in 1866, "just after a performance, in male attire, and swearing like a Gulf pirate, was very great." With the illusion forever shattered, he never again tried to deceive anyone about his gender, although he continued to appear professionally as a woman.

When Kingsley returned to San Francisco as Ella in 1867, his truth was known to all. Newspapers now advertised "Omar Kingsley in his great act as Ella Zoyara, acknowledged by all to be the most finished equestrian performance in the world." By 1870, however, he billed himself as "Omar Kingsley, Champion Rider of the World" and "rarely appeared as a female rider, doing so principally on the occasion of benefits." His last appearance in the city was in 1875.

The *San Francisco Chronicle* remembered Kingsley with affection, praising his skills as both an equestrian and female impersonator and fondly recalling the star's ability to "impersonate female character in a manner that almost defied detection." Not until some years later did the paper decide, "His long masquerade seemed to have changed his whole nature from a masculine to a feminine one. He was as emotional and capricious as any woman and had the temper of a virago." A changing world was finding new threats to masculinity.

Right: Twice married (to two women at the same time), William Lingard considered himself to be a quick-change artist rather than a female impersonator. *Photograph by J. Gurney & Son. Wikimedia Commons.*

Below: Vaudevillian and minstrel Paul Vernon appeared multiple times in *Houseworth's Celebrities*, an extensive series of photographs that showed famous personalities of the time. *Bancroft Library, University of California, Berkeley.*

PAUL VERNON.
Houseworth's Celebrities, 12 Montgomery St., San Francisco.

PAUL VERNON.
Houseworth's Celebrities, 12 Montgomery St., San Francisco.

William Horace Lingard, né William Redworth Needham (1837–1927), made his San Francisco debut in 1870, accompanied by his wife, Alice Dunning, and his sister Dickie Lingard. Unlike Ella, he specialized in lightning costume changes, "by which," one reviewer wrote, "Venus was changed into Adonis." Never exclusively a female impersonator, "this man," the reviewer noted, "had a great variety of costly dresses, such as are worn by females, as well as clothing worn by the male fraternity." Legally, Lingard could wear his professional apparel only inside the theater.

A few years later, female impersonator Paul Vernon became one of the most popular vaudevillians in San Francisco, "a city already known for its taste in transvestite performance." Critics praised his "wonderful female impersonations." He joined Haverly's United Mastodon Minstrels as a "burlesque prima-donna" in 1880, earning thirty-five dollars a week. Among other roles, he was Olivette in *Olivette*—his singing "deservedly applauded," wrote one reviewer—and the heroine Lean-O'er-Her (née Leonora) in the troupe's travesty of *Il Trovatore*. He also appeared as the Goddess of Liberty.

In an era when virtually every minstrel show featured cross-dressing men, Vernon and his many counterparts were readily accepted onstage by their almost entirely male audiences. As long as their characters were innocuous and inoffensive or obvious and farcical, no one saw a challenge to traditional masculine roles and identifications; any personal femininity was explained away as "a very finished piece of acting." Only portrayals of "a certain class of effeminate young man" in male clothes were considered distasteful.

San Francisco's own Bothwell Browne (1877–1947)—he was born in Denmark, raised in San Jose—found more limited acceptance because he challenged convention. His production of *Miss Jack* in 1911 failed because the entire cast consisted of cross-dressing actors and actresses. He had more success with his famed vaudeville act of exotic dances and his appearance as Cleopatra in *The Vampire of the Nile*. *Variety* called it "the best staged, produced, costumed, and elaborate dancing turn that ever left the Pacific Coast." Others found it too sensual and too seductive, raising unsettling questions about gender and sexual attraction.

Browne's greatest triumph was as the star of Mack Sennett's 1919 comedy *Yankee Doodle in Berlin*. Playing Captain Bob White, he impersonates a woman who seduces members of the German high command, including the Kaiser, to get vital military secrets. To promote the film, Browne toured the big-time vaudeville theaters and finally "played the Palace" in New York as a

Opposite: Many found female impersonator Bothwell Browne's stage appearances to be just a little too convincing for their own comfort, raising unsettling questions about gender and sexual attraction. *Author's collection.*

Left: At the peak of his career, between 1910 and 1925, Julian Eltinge, a.k.a. Mr. Lillian Russell, was one of the highest-paid actors in America. *Billy Rose Theatre Division, The New York Public Library.*

headliner, the most coveted booking in American vaudeville. After a decline in theater bookings during the 1920s, he left performance to teach dance in San Francisco.

No one, however, eclipsed the accomplishments of Julian Eltinge, who balanced convincing femininity onstage with comforting masculinity offstage for more than a quarter century. However ladylike he appeared in the theater, he and his publicists were always careful to explain that "his assumed womanliness was a triumph of art over virile nature." Sime Silverman, editor of *Variety*, called him "as great a performer as there is today."

Dorothy Parker seemed to agree when she wrote "A Musical Comedy Thought," for the June 1916 issue of *Vanity Fair*:

> *My heart is simply melting at the thought of Julian Eltinge;*
> *His alter ego, Vesta Tilley, too.*
> *Since our language is so dexterous, let us call them ambi-dexterous—*
> *Why hasn't this occurred before to you?*

When not working, Julian Eltinge publicized his masculinity, posing indecorously with actor Donald Crisp and director Cecil B. DeMille between takes for *The Clever Mrs. Carfax* in 1917. *Film Stills Archive, The Museum of Modern Art, New York.*

Not everyone was enchanted, of course. "When Julian Eltinge entered," W.C. Fields quipped, "women went into ecstasies over him. Men went into the Smoking Room."

His debut performance in San Francisco, a triumph, was in 1905. He returned in 1912 in *The Fascinating Widow*, his signature part and greatest success. As a famous female illusionist, he published the *Julian Eltinge Magazine of Beauty Hints and Tips* for women—if he could become a lovely lady, he asserted, then they certainly could—endorsed a line of corsets and marketed his own cold cream, liquid whiting and powder. Lured to Hollywood, he was the most successful female impersonator in film until Lassie.

PART III

PUBLIC LIVES, PRIVATE LOVES

CHAPTER 10

GERTRUDE AND ALICE: ICONS OF MODERNITY

I n English or in French, Gertrude Stein's native and adopted languages, the word to describe her is the same: formidable. She possessed one of the most creative and influential minds of the twentieth century, such that her brilliance mystified and confounded many—including, at times, herself. "It will take her years to understand the things she's said tonight," Alice Toklas, never known for cattiness, remarked after one soiree.

Born in Allegheny, Pennsylvania, in 1874, Gertrude Stein was raised in Oakland, California. She attended Radcliffe College and Johns Hopkins University before moving to Paris in 1903. Her father's success as a businessman—among other interests, he was a director of San Francisco's Market Street Railway—gave her the financial independence to make France her home, which she did for the rest of her life. She returned to the United States only once. It was with Toklas in October 1934 for a six-month visit and lecture tour.

Toklas also came from a prosperous background. Her paternal grandfather had been a rabbi in Poland. Her father, Ferdinand, immigrated to San Francisco in 1863, where he married Emma Levinsky in 1876. Alice was born there the next year, her brother, Clarence, ten years later. They moved to Seattle in 1890, where Alice attended Mount Rainier Seminary and the University of Washington, before returning to San Francisco six years later. After the Great Earthquake and Fire of 1906, Toklas moved to Paris.

Stein and Toklas met in Paris through a mutual friend in the fall of 1907. By the following summer, they were deeply in love, their lives entwined

Gertrude Stein (*right*) and Alice Toklas were the most famous lesbian couple in the world when Man Ray took their photograph in Paris, circa 1922. *National Portrait Gallery, Washington, D.C.*

in every conceivable way until Stein's death in 1946. Stein often said the stability of their home life, where Toklas took on all domestic responsibilities, enabled her to make her far-reaching contributions to the literary arts. They became the most famous openly lesbian couple in the world, their thirty-eight-year relationship a role model of what was possible for generations of women who love women.

Thoroughly involved with the avant-garde in Paris, Stein became a patron of Pablo Picasso, Henri Matisse and other major artists when they were still unknown. Her intent was to do for language what they did for visual arts, and she brought cubism to writing, deconstructing everyday images and ideas by first separating words from their usual meanings and then rearranging the traditional elements, forms and patterns of expression.

Stein simply was one of the most revolutionary experimenters with language of the last one hundred years, challenging literary tradition at every turn. Why must stories, she asked, have beginnings, middles and ends? Why must plays have acts of equal length? Why can autobiography be written only by the person whose life story is being told? Why must key words not be repeated in a sentence or a paragraph? Why must words be used only in their usual ways?

Even when she used traditional forms, she broke their rules. Written in 1911 but not published until 1922, "Miss Furr and Miss Skeene" tells a story with a beginning, middle and end, although it reads unlike any story before it. In barely 2,100 words, Stein creates two vivid personalities, describes their world in detail and unfolds the discovery of their love for each other, while at the same time portraying one of the first lesbian couples in English literature as "regular" and completely normal.

She does this with plain, direct language, using simple words over and over to invent a different way to express thought. The word "gay" appears 136 times, one of the first instances in print where it describes a homosexual relationship. Juxtaposing it with other words, she creates its modern meaning and a new understanding of the love of two women for each other.

Three years later, Stein published *Tender Buttons*. One of the great avant-garde experiments in verse, the work uses everyday words—like those in its wonderful punning title—put together in ways that challenge their usual meanings and create new ones for them. Critics variously called it "a masterpiece of verbal Cubism, a modernist triumph, a spectacular failure, a collection of confusing gibberish and an intentional hoax."

Stein insisted her work was completely realistic. She once explained, "I used to take objects on a table…and create a word relationship between the word and the things seen." It was therefore a challenging process to answer her simple, underlying question: How does language actually construct the world we know? Those who found the writings of Edgar Guest demanding did not care for Stein's work, which included novels, plays, poetry, libretti, detective stories, film scripts, magazine articles, even theoretical text.

Another literary form Stein reinvented was autobiography, writing the life story of her wife from her point of view and in her voice. *The Autobiography of Alice B. Toklas* created another new genre. One of her most accessible works, it became a bestseller when it was published in 1933; it is still in print. Only *Wars I Have Seen* (1945), her memoir of the Second World War, was more widely read during her lifetime, even becoming a selection of the Book-of-the-Month Club.

Stein was seen as an important thinker almost from the beginning of her long and influential career, and her writings continue to be underappreciated in the fragmented, deconstructed, cubist civilization that she recognized existed years before it did. Whether read or simply read about, however, she remains one of the most original and influential minds of the last one hundred years, a formidable figure who helped to shape the spirit and expression of our world of now.

Toklas stayed on in Paris after Stein died in 1946. *The Alice B. Toklas Cookbook* appeared in 1954, containing artist Brion Gysin's famous recipe for hashish fudge; Toklas claimed that she never tested the recipe and did not know about its then-unusual ingredient. A second cookbook, *Aromas and Flavors of Past and Present*, with less controversial fare, was published in 1958. Five years later, her own autobiography of herself, *What Is Remembered*, appeared. She died in 1967.

CHAPTER 11

THE FRENCH BEETHOVEN AND LA CREATICE

I n 1915, San Francisco welcomed the world to the grandest festivities in its history. Intended to salute the completion of the Panama Canal, the Panama-Pacific International Exposition much more celebrated the renaissance of the city after the Great Earthquake and Fire of 1906. More than eighteen million people attended, including two world-famous members of what we now call our LGBTQ+ communities: the venerated composer Camille Saint-Saëns (1835–1921) and the renowned dancer La Loïe Fuller (1862–1928).

In May 1915, Saint-Saëns, then almost eighty years old, traveled the 5,500 miles from his home in France to San Francisco to debut his new work, *Hail! California*, commissioned by the exposition as its official composition. Typically, he favored more exotic destinations in North Africa, where he went, by his own admission, as much for the waifs as for the waters.

Saint-Saëns was feted throughout his visit, although he did not attend any parties here dressed as soprano Caroline Carvalho, who had sung Marguerite at the premiere of Gounod's *Faust* and for which impersonation Saint-Saëns was famous among dear friends in Paris; no composer since Mozart wore a wig to greater effect. Neither did he dance in a tutu, which he reputedly effected to entertain fellow composer Pyotr Tchaikovsky, a frequent visitor to the City of Light.

Hail! California premiered at the exposition in Festival Hall, which stood near what is now the intersection of Pierce Street and Toledo Way. It delighted the audience of four thousand but never entered the repertoire.

Right: Nicknamed the French Beethoven, Camille Saint-Saëns composed *Hail! California* especially for San Francisco's Panama-Pacific International Exposition. *Photograph by Pierre Petit, 1900. National Library of France.*

Below: Saint-Saëns conducted three concerts of his own compositions at the exposition on June 19, June 24 and June 27, 1915, assisted by eighty musicians and a mixed chorus of three hundred voices. *Author's collection.*

Saint-Saëns's visit did result in a more enduring musical legacy, however, in his *Élégie, Op. 143*, composed during his visit.

Saint-Saëns was still in the city when La Loïe Fuller, arguably the most acclaimed dancer in the world, appeared at the exposition. Before there was Isadora Duncan, whom she encouraged, or Ruth St. Denis or Martha Graham, there was Fuller, a natural and spontaneous performer whose ideas and innovations became the foundations of modern dance.

Born Marie Louise Fuller in 1862 near Chicago, Illinois, she began her theatrical career as a professional child actress and later performed as a skirt dancer in vaudeville and circus shows. She became well known in America but felt that her work was not being taken seriously by the public. That changed when she moved to Europe, where her 1892 debut at the Folies Bergère in Paris brought her international celebrity.

As a woman who loved women, Fuller had little interest in appearing as a tutued ballerina locked in her prince's loving gaze, surrounded by admiring male courtiers as an object of masculine desire. No dying swans, no unrequited peasant girls, no suffering Cinderellas for her. Instead, she transmuted herself into a kinetic sculpture onstage, presenting what critics described as "transformative imagery of hypnotic beauty" and "the dizziness of soul made visible by artifice."

To accomplish this, Fuller created a new methodology of movement and presentation. She devised her own costumes, made from yards and yards of gossamer-thin silk. She designed her own lighting, performing in a rainbow of colors provided by revolving discs with tinted gels, another of her innovations. She did away with scenery, illuminated the stage from below, projected images onto her clothing and choreographed shadows and silhouettes. Except for the music, every aspect of her performance was hers.

Long separated from her husband—he was wed to her and two other women when she left him—she found personal happiness with Gabrielle Sorère (née Bloch), a member of her company, who became her lifelong companion, manager and artistic collaborator and the cofounder of her all-woman dance company in 1907.

Fuller and Sorère were always innovating; their final work together was the 1921 film *The Lily of Life*, which Sorère directed. It was one of the first motion pictures to use a negative print to distinguish reality from illusion. A couple for more than two decades, they were parted only by Fuller's death in 1928.

Fuller first appeared in San Francisco at the California Theater on November 23, 1893, the beginning of a week of sold-out performances;

La Loïe Fuller first appeared in San Francisco at the California Theater in 1893, where she sold out every performance. *Photograph by Isaiah Taber, San Francisco. Jerome Robbins Dance Division, The New York Public Library.*

a month later, she returned to participate in a benefit for the Relief Fund sponsored by the *San Francisco Chronicle*, which designated her "queen of dancers."

Her visit in 1915 was to choreograph the Panama-Pacific International Exposition's opening day dance procession. Unfortunately, her dancers became completely lost in the throng of 150,000 residents and visitors who joined them on their way to the fairgrounds.

When Fuller came to the exposition in 1915, she was fifty-three years old and only rarely performed in public. For the celebration, however, she appeared onstage with her troupe of Parisian students, whom she called her "Muses," in a series of dance recitals that included *Prelude à l'après-midi d'un faune* by Debussy and Grieg's *Peer Gynt* (Fuller took the role of the Mountain King). The ensemble later danced under the rotunda of the Palace of Fine Arts, hoping to raise money to preserve it after the fair closed.

Fuller helped to leave another lasting contribution to the city through the generosity of her great friend Alma de Bretteville Spreckels. The two women met in Paris in 1914, where Fuller introduced Alma to the sculptor

Auguste Rodin. Alma purchased a number of his works directly from him, which she put on display in the exposition's French Pavilion, a three-quarter-scale version of France's Palace of the Legion of Honor.

To house her collection after the exposition closed, Alma had an almost exact replica of the pavilion built in Lincoln Park, a copy of a copy, which opened in 1924. Fuller herself continues to be an influence on contemporary dance.

CHAPTER 12

THE FABULOUS BAKER STREET BOYS

I n late February 1918, the people of San Francisco learned, for the first time, that their city was home to a community of men who desired other men in all relationships, including sexual intimacy. During the next six months, they would discover that these individuals came together from many of the different ethnic, religious and cultural groups that formed the mosaic of the urban life they knew. They seemed like all men in the city in every way except one: they sought other men for sex.

What became the Baker Street vice scandal initially had nothing to do with such "shocking revelations." It began when the military police from the Presidio arrested a soldier at one of the two residential flats at 2525 and 2527 Baker Street. Taken back to the base for questioning, he admitted that civilians and soldiers were meeting at the flats, less than two blocks from the Presidio's western wall, for sex.

The military, without legal jurisdiction in the city, called the San Francisco police and then returned with them to Baker Street. For the next ten days, they brought both soldiers and civilians to the residences for questioning, keeping them there while they completed their investigation. Eventually, some two dozen men "in various walks of life" and from all parts of the country were indicted by the grand jury for "immoral practices," "unspeakable felonies" and "violating the statutes that govern morality"; many more were named but not charged.

When the daily newspapers began reporting about what they termed the "Baker Street vice ring," they could not tastefully include information regarding the sexual acts or even the statutes the men were accused of violating. The *San Francisco Examiner* stated simply that they "are alleged to be members of a 'club,' the character of which, the authorities state, justified the drastic action taken." In the *San Francisco Chronicle*, the "club" was "a rendezvous for a large number of vicious men."

In their teens, twenties, thirties and forties, these San Franciscans did not seem to fit their contemporaries' view of "men who do with men." Contrary to popular stereotypes of the time and descriptions by many historians since, none dressed like women or typically displayed feminine characteristics, used rouge or other cosmetics in public or expressed their sexuality by paying heterosexual men for the privilege of pleasuring them.

Not isolated in any way from each other or the society around them, the men sought out like-minded men for company as well as intimacy. They knew where and how to meet like-minded individuals for brief, often anonymous sexual adventures, but they also dated, lived together as friends, became deeply involved romantically and even shared homes as couples in long-term relationships that lasted decades.

Their social backgrounds were remarkably diverse. Some of them had barely finished the sixth grade, while others were graduates of prestigious universities. They worked at many trades and professions, from farmer to tailor to salesman to financier, yet none saw anything unusual about an unemployed office assistant and a prominent nabob enjoying an evening together or even becoming dear friends. They formed overlapping circles of community, fraternized across class lines, gathered at one another's homes and spent time together that was not sexual.

They knew their erotic desires were different from those of other men, but they also believed their feelings were natural and normal, at least for them, whatever the reason. Their sexuality shaped how they saw themselves and others, where they went to meet, whom they sought and what they did in friendship and intimacy. Their awareness formed their lives.

Like gay men before and since, the men of the Baker Street scandal knew where and how to find each other. Many met through mutual friends. Others met riding on a trolley, looking in a shop window, strolling along the street, sitting in a hotel bar, browsing in a store, attending the theater or visiting downtown alleys, bathhouses and other places known for casual, often anonymous, sexual encounters. As one explained, "It was a natural consequence that I come in contact with men who were congenial."

Many of those men were gay in almost every modern sense of the term except their use of the term itself. They knew they were sexually attracted

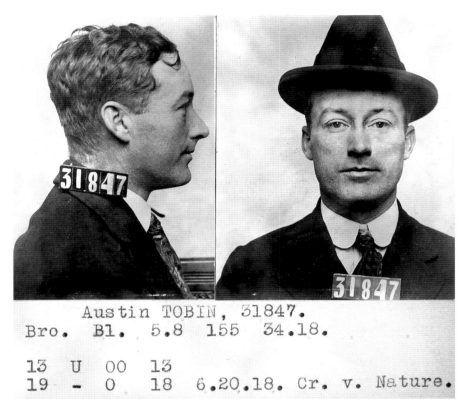

Austin Tobin received a sentence of five years to life for his intimacy with Howard Wilson. He was paroled in 1924. *San Quentin State Prison Records, California State Archives, Sacramento, California.*

to other men—not only physically, but also socially and emotionally—and they were aware that their desires were inherent and instinctive. Although the concept of sexual orientation did not yet exist, the men believed their feelings were natural and normal, at least for them, whatever the reason.

"We are all of a temperamental nature," Clarence Thompson told investigators at Baker Street, using the term for gay men then common. Investigators asked Austin Tobin, "Have [your] affairs always been of that sort? You are temperamental in that particular way?" He replied simply, "Yes." John Bosworth had known about himself from childhood, stating, "This temperamental character is or was very largely something natural, a condition of mine of which I was in nowise responsible, something born."

During his interrogation, Laurel Yeamans also admitted he had been temperamental "ever since I can remember." So did Garwood Simons:

Q Have you been temperamental since you can first remember?
A Yes, sir.
Q When did you first begin to feel inclinations in that matter?
A Approximately sixteen and a half...but before that I knew, inheritably
      [sic] that I had some spirit in me that wanted to come out.

Tebe Creighton not only understood who he was, but he also openly objected to the army persecuting him for it. He was someone who "entirely lacks any sense of shame," his medical examiners told the court. In addition, they reported he had "a feeling of resentment at the unfairness of the law in taking special cognizance of sexual perversions and imposing extra severe punishments for them."

Such understanding escaped the authorities. The army court-martialed six soldiers for "unnatural copulation." Bosworth received a prison term of ten years at hard labor. Howard Wilson's sentence was six years. Creighton and Yeaman were each given five years. All served their terms at McNeil's Island Federal Penitentiary in Washington. Walter Frank, behind bars at

Sentenced to six years in prison for his "affair" with Austin Tobin, Howard Wilson was paroled in 1919, five years before Tobin left San Quentin. *McNeil Island Penitentiary Records, National Archives.*

Walter Schneider (misspelled "Schnider" on his Department of Corrections record), given a sentence of five years to life, was paroled from San Quentin in 1924 but forbidden to return to San Francisco. *San Quentin State Prison Records, California State Archives, Sacramento, California.*

Alcatraz, was freed in December 1918 because he was ill. Simons was found not guilty of unspeakable acts but convicted of telling an officer about them and then dishonorably discharged.

The civil courts were even more intolerant. For his intimacy with Wilson, Tobin was given a sentence of "five years to life" and sent to San Quentin. Walter Schneider received the same sentence, although the man he was convicted of knowing was never arraigned. Those indicted for other sexual crimes were more fortunate. They had their cases dropped in 1919 when the state supreme court ruled that the statute making fellatio illegal four years earlier was unconstitutional; the legislature quickly corrected the "flaw in the law."

After they completed their prison terms, the two soldiers from the Bay Area returned to their families: Walter Frank to his wife in San Jose, Garwood Simons to his parents' home in Laurel Heights, San Francisco.

John Bosworth, who before his arrest had been considered for officers' training school, returned to the Bay Area to work at the U.S. Public Health Service Hospital in Menlo Park. The others went back to their homes before the war.

Although some of the civilians moved away when their legal troubles concluded—their parole boards forbade Tobin and Schneider from returning to San Francisco—most remained in the city after the charges against them were dropped. All the men who were employed by others were fired from their jobs, but many found similar work with different companies. Those who had their own businesses continued in them for many more years. The scandal apparently did not force any of them to close their firms.

The life of one of the men ended tragically in yet another scandal. Fired from his job after six years with the Santa Fe Railway, Quay Barnett eventually found employment as a clerk at the Vegetable Exchange and soon was promoted to traffic manager. In 1922, one of "four bachelors" at a

Laurel Yeamans served not quite one year and three months of his five-year sentence for "unnatural copulation" with Oscar Frank, who was never indicted. *McNeil Island Penitentiary Records, National Archives.*

"week-end party" in Mill Valley, he was shot and fatally wounded by his host, Rafael de Bettencourt, an artist and San Francisco interior decorator.

San Franciscans John (or Joseph) Doyle, a former captain in the British army, and Thomas Callahan, a bartender, the other two "members of the party," who witnessed "what occurred immediately prior to the shooting," initially claimed that when Bettencourt "did the killing," he had acted deliberately. In court, however, "testimony that the shooting…was accidental was offered by all witnesses called," and Bettencourt was acquitted.

The Baker Street scandal affected temperamentals in San Francisco for decades to come. Since the gold rush, law enforcement had generally ignored them unless someone complained. During the 1920s, for the first time, the police deliberately began to seek them out, using decoys and undercover officers to provide their own complainants and their own witnesses—sometimes the same individuals—who were immediately credible in court.

By the time persecution of gay men in California peaked in the 1960s, the Baker Street "vice club" scandal had been mostly forgotten by everyone except the men once caught up in it. A few, by good fortune, were still living in 1973 when the American Psychiatric Association decided they in fact were not pathological and neurotic and two years later when the state finally repealed the laws telling them who they could love and who they could be.

CHAPTER 13

THE CASE FOR SEXUAL LIBERTY

The two defendants probably never realized they were making history. They simply wanted to find a way out of a difficulty that could bring them up to fifteen years in prison. Even so, appealing their arrests for having oral sex to the state supreme court, Clarence Lockett and Don Alvarado Gono became the first men to successfully challenge a California state law that forbade sexual intimacy between consenting adults.

In 1915, California's state legislature added "a new section to the penal code, to be numbered 288a, relating to sex perversions and defining the same to be felonies." For the first time, it prohibited "acts technically known as fellatio and cunnilingus," the only occasion those words would be used in a statute passed in the United States.

Section 288a created legal confusion almost immediately. No one seemed to understand what it was the legislature had outlawed. In 1916, an appellate court, in the case of *People v. Carrell*, overturned J.E. Carrell's conviction for performing fellatio because the term describing his crime was not used or understood by the public. Carrell himself did not know what it meant. Apparently, neither did anyone else: he had been charged with committing fellatio on a woman. The statute, however, remained intact.

Two years later, San Francisco police arrested William Soady for violating the new law. Although an army private stationed at the Presidio, he was jailed as a civilian, his "sin against decency" having occurred before he went into uniform. While awaiting trial, his attorney petitioned for a writ of habeas corpus, arguing that Soady was being held illegally because Section 288a was unconstitutional.

Above: After his conviction for his "sin against decency" was overturned on appeal, William Soady returned to military service. He was honorably discharged at the end of the Great War. *Ancestry.com.*

Opposite: Clarence Lockett was nineteen years old when, in 1914, a jury convicted him of committing grand larceny "while made up as a woman." *San Quentin State Prison Records, California State Archives, Sacramento, California.*

Eventually, Soady's case went up to the state supreme court. His position was simple. The legislature, of course, had every right to enact a statute "tending to the suppression of sins against decency." Section 288a, however, by using a Latin word—"fellatio"—to designate, but not to define, the behavior it forbade, contradicted California's constitution, which required that all laws be written in English. Therefore, the statute was invalid and unenforceable.

Soady lost his appeal. The court ruled that Section 288a was viable because it obviously was enacted to ban "sex perversions." Its intent, the majority claimed, made its meaning "clear in context and purpose," whether or not anyone knew the term specifically. Soon after, on its own motion, the court granted Soady a rehearing, but by then, the charges against him had been dismissed.

Until his case came to trial, no one, apparently, noticed that Soady's "grievous lapse" was in 1914, before the legislature forbade "the specific act," as the *San Francisco Call and Post* described it, so he had not broken any law. With his mother sitting in the courtroom, a jury acquitted him on the recommendation of the assistant district attorney.

Soady had also committed his "sin" before he enlisted in the army, so he was additionally innocent of violating the military code of conduct. His status as a soldier, if not his reputation, remained "without official blemish," even though the army knew he enjoyed sex with men, which it forbade. He stayed in uniform, without any apparent injury to martial morale or effectiveness, until the end of his military service, when he received an honorable discharge.

The next two cases challenging Section 288a came before the state supreme court in late 1918. The first concerned Lockett, twenty-three. The second involved Gono, who was forty-two when he was "charged with practicing immorality"; when the police raided his room in a Polk Street hotel, reported the *San Francisco Chronicle* on April 5, 1918, they found a book containing the names of thirty soldiers in one company at the Presidio. Although filed separately by different attorneys, the justices decided to rule on the cases together.

Lockett had been in trouble with the authorities before. Born in Waco, Texas, on April 26, 1895, he was nineteen years old when police arrested him for robbing "Otto Achzen of San Francisco while made up as a woman," according to the *Oakland Tribune* for October 27, 1914. Sent to San Quentin, where he worked as a cell tender, he served two years, eight months, of a three-and-a-half-year sentence. Exactly nine months after his release on September 13, 1917, he was appealing his arrest for "sexual perversion."

Lockett was fortunate to have Oscar Hudson as his attorney, the first African American admitted to the California bar. Hudson argued that Section 288a, not being entirely in English, was "so indefinite and uncertain and unintelligible" that it failed to inform the accused of "the nature and cause of the accusation." This time, the court agreed, invalidating the law for technical reasons; it did not endorse the "immoral behavior" it once again made legal.

After their cases were dismissed, both Gono and Lockett continued to live in San Francisco. Gono, who had been a salesman for leaf tobacco dealers H & L London (owned by brothers Henry and Louis) when he was arrested, opened his own business, manufacturing eucalyptus novelties with his partner, James Goodwin. The two men both worked and lived together.

Barely six months after his conviction was overturned, however, police arrested Lockett again, this time on Van Ness Avenue, for disturbing the peace. Under the headline "Siren Causes Downfall of Negro 'Fairy'," the *Chronicle* reported on July 16, 1919, that "Lockett, a colored entertainer" had "rented himself out to entertain a home party," wearing a costume consisting of goblin's slippers, a pink shirt with "little white wings where they are supposed to be worn by fairies" and a crown made of a golden topknot.

The *Chronicle* did not mention Lockett's earlier encounters with the law. It was having too much fun mocking his appearance and his behavior. "He was standing in the middle of the street when an automobile siren shrieked behind him. He started to run. The siren went again. He ran faster," passing "a policeman who gave chase" and then "fired a shot in the air to halt Lockett," although "that only gave the latter more speed." After Lockett "tripped and fell," he was arrested for disturbing the peace.

The *Oakland Tribune* reported the encounter with similar flippancy in an article it titled "Fairy in Flight Disturbs Peace," which appeared on page one of its evening edition for July 16. "When a negro 'fairy,' attired in a pink shirt, green tights, wings, and goblin slippers, runs wildly down a street, scaring horses and what few topers [men who wear top hats] are able to carry the 'red stuff' on their hips, then that fairy is disturbing the peace."

Lockett, the paper explained, had been entertaining at a party in "fairylike paraphernalia" when he was "given wine, which is no drink for a fairy." On his way home, "an auto horn tooted behind, and he fled down the street, a vision fearful in its shock to the optic nerves of three horses and a policeman [who] recovered from his amazement before the horses did, gave chase, and 'pinched' the vision."

The victory Gono and Lockett achieved was short-lived. In 1921, the legislature passed a new statute, written entirely "in plain English," that made "the act of copulating the mouth of one person with the sexual organ of another" illegal. It was a busy year for the guardians of other people's morality; the legislature also approved a measure that banned "any act… which openly outrages public decency."

Whatever that was, it gave police permission to arrest people for virtually anything. Both laws remained in effect for many years, disrupting lives, imprisoning people and surrounding human interactions with fear and guilt.

CHAPTER 14

CLARKSON CRANE: CRUISING BETWEEN THE WARS

When Clarkson Crane published *The Western Shore*, his first novel, in 1925, it was notable for many reasons. It was the first book from a mainstream American press whose characters openly speculated about each other's sexuality—their "tendencies in love"—and wondered whether or not they were "queer." It presented its gay characters not as stereotypes but as individuals who came from different backgrounds, "a gallery of credible human beings." None was a villain, corrupting the innocent around him. Nobody met a tragic ending.

Born in Chicago in 1894, Crane moved to California with his family in 1911. He graduated from UC Berkeley in 1916. After the United States entered the Great War the next year, he joined Section 586 of the U.S. Army Ambulance Corps, made up largely of UC students and recent alumni. For his bravery at Aisne and Champagne in 1918, the French army awarded him the Croix de Guerre.

Crane returned to California after the war, wanting to be a writer, but found he could not support himself. In 1924, he returned to France. Living on a small stipend provided by an aunt, he settled into a humble hotel on the Left Bank in Paris. There he took up the bohemian life of an expatriate and, drawing on his experiences as a Berkeley student, completed *The Western Shore*.

The book was remarkably frank for the period, asking, "Who is gay?" and "How can you tell?" Probably the "fellow [who] had a squeaky voice, plucked his eyebrows, and always had his left palm against his hip." Not the man who was "not effeminate. [His] voice was very soft, not at all squeaky; he rarely touched any one he knew; and frequently kept his eyes averted.…

Clarkson Crane (*left*) and his life partner, Clyde Evans, were a couple for more than forty-seven years. *Clarkson Crane Papers (1997-46), GLBT Historical Society.*

Naw…'he's not queer.'" Earlier novelists did not have questions. They simply presented stereotypes.

Many of Crane's novels are washed with homoeroticism, although his most specific is *The One and the Many*. Written between 1948 and 1953, it tells the story of a young man's journey of self-discovery in San Francisco between the world wars. Even then, Crane writes, "There were plenty of young homos drifting around town with whom I could have sex." Whatever its literary merit—it was never published—the narrative is invaluable as a documentary of a time when same-sex relationships could lead to long prison terms.

The book is rich with information about how men thought about themselves. At the time, many believed homosexuality was a perversion or a mental illness, but Crane's narrator is very comfortable with being gay. He believes it is normal for him. "As far back as I could remember I had always been attracted to boys," he says.

"Expert opinion" simply was wrong, Crane's narrator says, but "two books gave much clearer understanding of my nature: *Leaves of Grass* and *The Intermediate Sex*," by Edward Carpenter. "The need for concealment was the only aspect of homosexual life that I disliked. Otherwise, I felt quite satisfied to be what I was, and I would not have wanted to change my nature, even if that had been possible."

There were no bars, clubs or organizations then, but like-minded men still found each other. Crane's narrator meets someone in the library who brings him into his circle of friends. As he becomes more aware of himself and the world around him, he discovers there are many men—and women— who feel as he does about same-sex intimacy. He also finds the public places where men go to meet and be with each other.

Crane and Evans met at Ocean Beach (*foreground*), just across the Great Highway from Fleishhacker Pool (*center*), now site of the San Francisco Zoo. The photograph is circa 1930. *OpenSFHistory/wnp70.0495.*

One popular "cruising site" during the 1920s was Golden Gate Park, inside the Stanyan Street entrance. Another was the beach near what was then Fleishhacker Pool, now the site of the San Francisco Zoo, where Crane met Clyde Evans, his partner of forty-seven years. A third was among the "bohemians" in the Montgomery Block Building. Torn down to build the Transamerica Pyramid, it was for many years home to struggling artists and writers and almost certainly the seed that grew into San Francisco's LGBTQ+ community in North Beach.

Among the early gay-friendly places nearby was a "speak-easy in which homos were allowed to gather, if they were not rowdy." Called Martino's in *The One and the Many*, it was "above a grocery store on the second floor of a frame apartment house, and one was only supposed to be admitted if one had a card." Possibly the club was modeled on Finocchio's when it was over a store at Sutter and Stockton Streets.

During the same era, the city saw its first "gays only" bathhouses, where someone, Crane wrote, could have "a fabulous, but a perfectly fabulous time." His model may have been the Club Turkish Baths, which opened at 132 Turk in 1930. Some earlier bathhouses, known as places where like-minded men could meet each other, did not have an exclusively or even predominantly gay clientele.

More than any single way, Crane explains that "nearly always I have found my long-time friends in unexpected and perfectly ordinary places, or even in social gatherings where I was introduced to them—rarely in special places where homos gather." He was "always looking for someone who attracted me," he confesses. Fortunately, "I had developed the homo's all seeing eye," now known as "gaydar." *Plus ça change, plus c'est la même chose.*

CHAPTER 15

ELSA GIDLOW:
POET, PHILOSOPHER, INDEPENDENT WOMAN

Elsa Gidlow lived her life as she wanted, always: openly as an independent woman.

Gidlow was a poet, essayist, philosopher and humanist, and her first book, *On a Grey Thread* (1923), contained the first frankly lesbian love poetry published in the United States, written not only by and about a woman who loves women but also by one who identified herself as its author. Beginning with the "The Grey Thread," the first poem in the collection, she describes the different facets of her personal identity:

> *I have gay beads.*
> *A pale one to begin,*
> *A blue one for my painted dreams,*
> *And one for sin....*
>
> *For love an odd bead*
> *With a deep purple glow;*
> *A green bead for a secret thing*
> *That few shall know.*

Unlike the poets of earlier generations (Tennyson, Whitman, Dickinson), who used coded language to describe their deep affection for those of their own gender, Gidlow made no secret of the fact that she was writing about women loving each other. Both her own sexuality and "the direction of emotional attention" in her poems were undisguised:

> *Watch my Love in sleep:*
> *Is she not beautiful*
> *As a young flower at night*
> *Weary and glad with dew?*

The beliefs Gidlow shared in *On a Grey Thread* were far ahead of their time and contrary to its fundamental, traditional values. Not only was she openly admitting her sexual orientation and publicly advocating for same-sex intimacy—both purple and green were colors associated with homosexuality—she also endorsed open relationships:

> *You're jealous if I kiss this girl and that,*
> *You think I should be constant to one mouth?*
> *Little you know of my too quenchless drouth:*
> *My sister, I keep faith with love, not lovers.*

Born Elsie Alice Gidlow on December 29, 1898, in Hull, England, she moved with her family to Montreal, Canada, when she was fifteen. She knew who she was at an early age. In the fall of 1917, when she was still only eighteen, her letter to the *Montreal Daily Star* invited all interested individuals to join the first meeting of a writer's club she was starting. Among those who attended was Roswell George Mills, who became the first "openly gay" Canadian.

According to Gidlow, "He was beautiful. About nineteen, exquisitely made up, slightly perfumed, dressed in ordinary men's clothing but a little on the chi-chi side. And he swayed about, you know." Mills considered it his personal crusade to make people "understand that it was beautiful, not evil, to love others of one's own sex and make love with them." Because they were both interested in poetry and the arts, the two became fast friends.

Before moving to San Francisco in 1926, Elsa Gidlow worked for *Pearson's Magazine* in New York, where she had this stylish photograph of herself taken. *Elsa Gidlow Papers (1991-16), GLBT Historical Society.*

The year after they met, Gidlow and Mills founded *Les Mouches Fantastiques* (*The Fantastic Flies*), the first magazine published in North America not only to be written primarily by lesbians and gays but also to discuss their concerns and to celebrate them in its poetry and articles. No more than one hundred mimeographed copies of the early issues were produced, but those were passed from reader to reader. At least one reached an Episcopal priest living in South Dakota who then moved to Montreal to become Mills's lover.

Gidlow and Mills created five issues of the magazine before Gidlow moved to New York in 1920. Barely twenty-one, she was seeking greater opportunities to live as she pleased. She changed her name to Elsa, took a job with *Pearson's Magazine* and began a love affair with Violet (Tommy) Henry-Anderson, a Scottish golfer who was sixteen years her senior. "Tommy was able to tell me more than I had ever suspected of women's passionate, romantic involvement with one another," she wrote in 1986.

In 1926, she and Tommy left New York, sailing through the Panama Canal to San Francisco. Except for a year in Europe, visiting Mills and touring the continent, Gidlow continued to live in the Bay Area for the rest of her life. She and Tommy had been together thirteen years when Tommy died in 1935. "We were profoundly sure of our right to be as we were, to love and live in our chosen way, we were happy in it," Gidlow remembered.

Eventually, Gidlow moved to Fairfax, California, then a rural community some fifty miles north of the city. In 1946, she began corresponding with Isabel Grenfell Quallo, a Congolese-born British American who lived in New York. Gidlow invited her to visit, but Quallo was reluctant, explaining that "a woman who discovers she is a lesbian and is a visible member of a minority has three strikes against her." She arrived in 1947 only after Gidlow assured her that she lived in an open-minded community.

Gidlow was wrong. Soon the California senate's Subcommittee on Un-American Activities called her to testify about her membership in literary and political organizations that allegedly had communist affiliations. Although Gidlow, a philosophical anarchist, ideologically opposed communism, the group's 1948 report concluded she supported communist front organizations. She also was accused of "living with a colored woman and frequently entertaining Chinese people," charges she characterized as "damning evidence that I could not be a loyal American."

In 1954, she and Quallo moved onto a portion of a ranch she bought near Muir Woods with friends Mary and Roger Somers, which she named Druid Heights. It became both their home and a retreat for artists, writers, feminists and free spirits. Quallo returned East to care for family members in 1957, but Gidlow remained there for the rest of her life among guests and long-term residents, including Alan Watts, whose book *The Way of Zen* introduced Eastern philosophy and Zen Buddhism to many European and American readers.

Across her long creative career, Gidlow published fourteen books. Her last, *Elsa: I Come with My Songs*, the first autobiography of a lesbian published in the United States under its author's true name, appeared in 1986, the year she died. Although Gidlow saw herself first and foremost as a poet, the writer, publisher and activist Celeste West wrote that by then, she had added many more beads to her "grey thread" as a "radical feminist of the 'first wave'" who "fought life-long against class privilege, organized religion, and sexism, while fighting for all varieties of love and beauty."

CHAPTER 16

THE NIGHT THEY RAIDED TAIT'S

O n May 22, 1933, police raided San Francisco's first "pansy show." Although both female and male impersonators had been extremely popular in the city at least since the gold rush, the authorities were "shocked, shocked" to learn that some were appearing at Tait's. According to *Variety*, "Frisco's still a swaggering, tough town that likes its shows suggestive and its likker [*sic*] straight. But when it comes to pansy floor shows, that's a different matter."

Rae Bourbon was already a star when Joe Rosenberg invited him to bring his revue, *Boys Will Be Girls*, to Tait's, his club at 24 Ellis Street. The City Fathers were not amused. Shortly after the show began, reported *Variety*, "Capt. [Arthur] Layne stepped up to the stage, blew his whistle, and half a dozen coppers nabbed the boys." It was the first bar raid ever broadcast live on radio.

Local newspapers used direct, unambiguous language to report what happened. The *Oakland Tribune* simply stated that San Francisco police "broke up a midnight stage performance featuring five men impersonating women, while a crowd of diners looked on." The impersonators were charged with "the holding of a performance without a license."

Utilizing its famously—some would say notoriously—vivid language, *Variety* shared a much more flavorful account of the events with its readers. Running a page one article under a typically sassy, punning headline, "Rough Frisco Cops Send Pinched Boys to Women's Court," it described how "great big gorgeous policemen descended upon the spot and hauled off seven members

Born Hallie Board Waddell, Rae Bourbon's career as a female impersonator spanned four decades from the 1920s to the 1960s. *Photograph by John E. Reed, circa 1945. J. D. Doyle, Queer Music Heritage.*

of the 'Boys Will Be Girls' troupe, sticking 'em in a nasty old cell."

The raid took place right "after Rae Bourbon had done a Spanish dance in fem attire," the periodical reported. Apparently, the performers were given every consideration. The police "gave 'em time to take off their dresses" before they "then hustled 'em in the wagon which clanged to the station house with the gang of mascaraed, rouged, lipsticked impersonators who floored the tough Irish desk sergeant upon their entrance" at Central Station.

When he regained his composure, the sergeant "scheduled the hearing for the Women's court." There charges against all the performers were dismissed, but the police, hoping to force their closure, continued to raid the performances for next three nights. Finally, with the Board of Beverage Commissioners threatening to revoke his beer license, Rosenberg canceled the booking and brought in a "girl show." The cafe kept its permit, but business dropped considerably without "the pinches."

Bourbon and his troupe found new employment almost immediately. Less than a month after it closed in San Francisco, their "pinched pansy show" began an open-ended run—still as *Boys Will Be Girls*—at a roadhouse in Salt Lake City. According to *Variety*, the "show hasn't been bothered by [the] sheriff's office, and the natives are taking to the entertainment big." Bourbon returned to San Francisco three years later for the first of four appearances at Finocchio's between 1936 and 1946.

The raid did not stop other clubs in San Francisco from featuring female illusionists. Finocchio's, which began in 1929 as a speakeasy called the 201 Club at 406 Stockton Street, spotlighted them almost from the beginning. One night, journalist Jesse Hamlin wrote later, "A well-oiled customer got up and sang in a dazzling style that sounded just like Sophie Tucker. The crowd ate it up, and [owner Joe] Finocchio saw his future." The entertainment now featured a female impersonator. "Everyone came to see the show," he remembered. "And to drink."

Finocchio's survived Prohibition without much incident but was raided on July 20, 1936, because of what plainclothes "officers characterized as a vulgar parody given by one of the impersonators," even though they apparently had requested it. As part of a then-ongoing campaign against "lewd entertainers" in San Francisco, police detained several performers as well as owners Theresa and Joe Finocchio, whom they charged with "keeping a disorderly house" and "employment of entertainers on a percentage basis," an alleged scheme that dated to the days of the gold rush.

At their hearings, female impersonators Walter Hart and Carrol Davis received sentences of thirty days in the county jail for performing "songs offensive to the ears in public"; Eugene Countryman was given a thirty-day suspended sentence when he showed that he took no part in the singing. Charges against the other performers were dismissed. Proceedings against the Finocchios were dropped with a promise that entertainers would not mix with customers. A year after the raid, the club moved to 506 Broadway, where the new Finocchio's debuted on July 15, 1937.

Both Hart and Davis made the move to the new location. Hart became famous as "the Male Sophie Tucker" for his amazing impersonation of the singer; she would see his performances when she was in the city and occasionally sent him some of her gowns, which the local newspapers duly reported. Between shows, Davis, a gifted comedian, often entertained from behind the Theatre Bar in a tux, "proving," historian James Smith wrote, "that a man could look like a woman dressed like a man."

There was never anything small or secretive about Hart. A local celebrity, he was mentioned in Herb Caen's It's News to Me column in the *San Francisco Chronicle* after he was given "a pedigreed cocker spaniel… from a Pennis. [*sic*] matron of reputation" and when he was seen "buying a lady's fur coat at Sammy's—for hissel'n." Caen also reported when "Hart, the long-time queen bee at Finocchio's Italian Swish-Colony [*sic*] on B'way bought that handsome silver fox he's wearing from Sophie Tucker—for $1000," a bargain.

Other writers also included the doings of "the Finocchio he'man" in their articles, describing him as "the peroxided boy" or "the platinum blonde entertainer." They even reported when he dyed his hair in 1943 and was "no longer a blonde." "Believe us, his tresses are back to normal," wrote the Owl—but, he reassured readers, "he still sings in his lusty Sophie Tucker manner. We'd be disappointed if he ever changed that routine." He never did.

Left: Famous as "the Male Sophie Tucker," Walter Hart, who headlined at Finocchio's during the 1930s and 1940s, remained always a darling of local columnists. *Author's collection.*

Right: Karyl Norman, who billed himself as "the Creole Fashion Plate," was especially known for his two-octave vocal range and his glamorous gowns, most made by his mother. *Alchetron.*

During the sixty-two years it was in North Beach, Finocchio's headlined some of the most acclaimed female impressionists in the world. Karyl Norman, who billed himself as "the Creole Fashion Plate," was known for his gowns—mostly made by his mother, who traveled with him—and for his two-octave vocal range, which allowed him to move easily from baritone to coloratura soprano; apparently, he never knew he was called "the Queer Old Fashion Plate" behind his back.

After a career in vaudeville that began sometime before 1919 and included his headlining at the Palace Theatre in 1930 in an act called *Glorifying the American Boy-Girl*, he turned to "the smarter night clubs." Billing him as "the world's highest paid female impersonator"—he himself described what he did as "character impressions"—Norman debuted at Finocchio's as master of ceremonies on March 29, 1941. He also appeared in the club's show *Fashion Advice to Women*, singing "the numbers he made famous on two continents."

Also known for his wardrobe—one "that would make a debutante pale with envy," wrote the *Chronicle*—Tex Hendrix followed Norman as the club's master of ceremonies in August 1941. Advertised as "the Wild Texan who

Tamed the Gay White Way," he owned "1000 gowns. Nine trunks full of them," according to the paper, which he claimed was "the finest wardrobe of any impersonator of all time." Every night, he displayed a different one with each of his twelve appearances onstage.

Hart was a headliner at Finocchio's for almost fifteen years. When he left in July 1949, apparently because of a disagreement with Mrs. Finocchio, Caen wrote, "That's sort of like the last ferry leaving the Ferry Bldg." He moved on to Club Chi Chi and then to Ann's 440, where he and Davis were again together. He died in 1978.

Unlike Hart and Davis, who stayed in San Francisco, Bourbon spent much of his career on the nightclub circuit, probably touring more than any other female impersonator. He returned to the city often, headlining at Finocchio's 1936, 1941, 1943 and 1946, his last appearance there, when he was featured in the *Romance in Rhythm* revue. Over the years, his fans also saw him at the Club Savoy, the Seven Seas, Club Drift-In, the Gold Coast, Coffee Dan's and Club Chi Chi.

For many gays in the 1930s, '40s and '50s, especially in smaller cities and towns, Bourbon's almost certainly was the only drag act—and possibly the only publicly open gay man—they ever saw. Those who could not attend his live performances could listen to his comedy on the records he made—probably more than any other female impersonator—beginning in the 1930s. They included his first long-playing recording, *Yes, It Is Rae Bourbon*, that preserves two routines he did at Coffee Dan's around 1953.

Bourbon appeared on Broadway with Mae West as Florian, a role she wrote specifically for him, in *Catherine Was Great* (1944–45) and as Bowery Rose, a "pansy shoplifter," in her revival of *Diamond Lil* (1949–50)—he toured with her in both shows—and in a sold-out concert performance, *Don't Call Me Madam*, at Carnegie Hall in 1948 where, wrote one reviewer, "you could hardly claw your way thru a mob of very spectacular characters."

Bourbon's last years were unfortunate. He had difficulty finding bookings and struggled financially and personally. In 1968, he was convicted of being an accomplice to murder and sentenced to ninety-nine years in a Texas penitentiary. He died while still serving his term in 1971. Whether he was a good "role model" or not, at least during his heyday, he let other gay men know they were not alone.

CHAPTER 17

ESTHER ENG:
PIONEERING FILMMAKER AND FEMINIST

Even before the lights dimmed for the 1936 world premiere of *Sum Hun*, known also as *Heartaches*, the audience was ready for a unique experience: watching the first motion picture made in Hollywood with only Chinese actors portraying Chinese characters, produced and directed by Chinese filmmakers. Equally extraordinarily, one of its producers was a woman, Esther Eng, who would make film history again and again for the next dozen years as the only female producing and directing Chinese-language films anywhere.

Born Ng Kam-ha in San Francisco on September 24, 1914, Eng grew up in the heart of the city's Chinatown. As a teenager, she saw traditional Chinese opera at the Mandarin Theatre on Grant Avenue, performed by companies brought over from Canton, Shanghai and Hong Kong. Many of the leading actors became her friends, including Wai Kim-Fong, "the Chinese Sarah Bernhardt," who would star in three of Eng's films.

Now considered lost, *Sum Hun* launched Eng's career as a writer, producer, director and distributor of Chinese-language motion pictures. Set in San Francisco but filmed at a studio in Hollywood, it was shot in only eight days; two of its nine reels were in color. It made news even before it debuted when an article in the December 15, 1935 *Los Angeles Times* titled "All-Chinese Film Made" declared it the "first oriental production with sound finished in Hollywood."

After *Sum Hun*'s American debut, Eng and "her dear friend" Wai journeyed to Hong Kong for the film's international premiere. She made

film history a second time when Hong Kong's largest motion picture studio hired her to direct *National Heroine*. Its themes of patriotism, equality between women and men and "self-sacrifice as the ultimate proof of personal love" would recur often in her work.

Released in 1937, *National Heroine* told the story of a female pilot, played by Wai, fighting as an equal beside her male comrades for her country. Hugely successful, it received a "Certificate of Merit" from the Kwangtung Federation of Women's Rights. Eng directed four more films in two years, again making history with *It's a Women's World*, the first film made in Hong Kong with an all-female cast. A "broad critique of contemporary society" in the city, especially its treatment of women, it was another success.

Even as a celebrated public figure, Eng never made a secret of her love of women. Journalists who reported about her private life often referred to those with whom she was intimate as "bosom friends" or "good sisters," but in 1938, a writer for Hong Kong's *Sing Tao Daily News* openly admired her as "living proof of the possibility of same-sex love." The revelations did not hurt her in Hong Kong as they would have in Hollywood.

Because of the growing war in Asia, Eng returned to the United States in late 1939. The next year, she began work on *Golden Gate Girl*, the first feature-length Chinese-language film made in San Francisco, which premiered in May 1941 at Chinatown's Grandview Theatre. *Film Daily* thought it "surprisingly good," despite having a budget that "would about cover a Hollywood test." Now lost, it also made history as the first screen appearance of future international star Bruce Lee—as a baby girl.

Eng directed only three more films during the 1940s, all starring her "great and good friend" Sui Fei-Fei: *Blue Jade* (1947), *Back Street* (1948) and *Mad Fire, Mad Love* (1949), which she also wrote, the first Chinese-language color feature made in Hawaii. After more than a decade writing, producing, directing and distributing motion pictures, she retired from the business.

In 1950, Eng moved to New York, where she opened the Chinese restaurant Bo Bo with Sui and four other partners. The extremely influential and socially out *New York Times* food editor and restaurant critic Craig Claiborne gave it three stars in the 1966 edition of his *Guide to Dining Out in New York*. The only problem with the restaurant, he wrote, was that "at times

Opposite: Esther Eng, the first woman to produce and direct Chinese-language films anywhere, followed her accomplishments in motion pictures with an equally successful career as a restaurateur. *Photograph by Thomas Chan, San Francisco. Alchetron.*

Above: "Dear friend" Wai Kim-Fong, a Cantonese opera actress from the Grand Stage Theater, starred in the first film Eng produced in Hollywood and the first she directed in Hong Kong. *Women Film Pioneers Project.*

it is next to impossible to obtain a table," although he admitted "the fare is worth waiting for."

After more than a decade, Eng returned to filmmaking one last time in 1961 for *Murder in New York Chinatown*, which she codirected with Wu Peng. She opened two more restaurants, Esther Eng on Pell Street and Eng's Corner on Mott Street. She died on January 25, 1970, only fifty-five years old, successful in two professions not always welcoming to women and during an era when society was not especially accepting of same-sex intimacy.

Eng's list of accomplishments in motion pictures was extraordinary: the first Chinese American women to produce a motion picture in Hollywood, the first woman to direct a film in Hong Kong, the first woman to film in color. Working only for independent film studios, Eng lacked the resources to make "a major motion picture," but she also was free of the restrictions Hollywood imposed, able to be her authentic self at work and in her personal life.

During the years after San Francisco–born Dorothy Arzner, then America's foremost woman director, retired in 1943 and Ida Lupino received her first screen credit for directing in 1949, Eng was the only woman making commercial films in the United States. Unlike them, she was entirely self-taught; she had never worked in a motion picture studio before coproducing *Heartaches* and received no formal training before she directed *National Heroine*. Even more impressive, she was only twenty-two when her first movie premiered. Arzner had been thirty. Lupino would be thirty-one.

Sadly, many of Eng's films are now considered lost. Someday, however, a persistent archivist or a curious janitor will open a disused cabinet or a dusty storage box in an abandoned garage or a gloomy basement and come across unremembered reels of film that will return one or more of Eng's films to us and to their place in motion picture history. The lights will dim, and we will again witness the history she made.

CHAPTER 18

JACKIE MEI LING AND CHINATOWN'S FEMALE IMPERSONATORS

A s a dancer, Jackie Mei Ling (1914–2000) could do it all. During San Francisco's Golden Age of Nightclubs from the 1940s to the 1960s, he successfully appeared before the public in everything from formal attire to drag. Creative, eclectic and resourceful, "his dance routines," wrote the historian Anthony W. Lee, "neither followed a preferred model nor seemed to present any one particular style." He not only "choreographed complex dance sequences for himself and his partners, but also designed the various costumes for each of their performances."

Born in Utah, Mei Ling grew up in San Francisco's Chinatown. He became interested in dance at an early age and studied with Walton "Biggy" Biggerstaff (1903–1995) at his Jackson Street studio, at the Ballet Company of San Francisco and, very briefly, with Theodore Kosloff in Los Angeles. He was appearing in nearby San Fernando Valley with then-partner Jadin Wong when Charlie Low, owner of Forbidden City, invited them to appear in his club. They quickly became the night spot's featured performers.

Mei Ling introduced Biggerstaff to Low around 1940, and he became Forbidden City's principal choreographer and producer for the next fourteen years. Many of his creations showcased what members of the audience, mostly white tourists, imagined the "exotic orient" to be; some, like 1942's *The Girl in the Gilded Cage*, received extensive publicity in periodicals as diverse as the winking *Carnival/Show* and *Collier's Weekly*, then a widely read family magazine. Openly gay, Biggerstaff was survived by his "life companion" Charles E. Lindsley.

The *San Francisco Examiner* considered dancer and choreographer Jackie Mei Ling to be one of the "top Chinese artists" to appear in the city during the 1940s. *John Grau collection.*

According to Lee, all of Mei Ling's dance partners knew he was gay, too, which apparently bothered neither them nor the club owners. Public disclosure, however, would have damaged his image as one half of an elegant and romantic couple. When he appeared at Andy Wong's Shangri-La in 1942, his photograph graced the cover of the souvenir program twice, as himself with partner Kim Wong and unnamed as "the world's greatest female impersonator." Reviewing the show, however, the *San Francisco Examiner* revealed it was "Jack Mei Ling, impersonator and dancer."

He also was discreet when he appeared in drag at Finocchio's. "I had an agreement with them that if there were any Chinese in the audience, I wouldn't dance," he told the historian and filmmaker Arthur Dong in an interview. "I didn't want [my family] to see me at Finocchio's." In 1946, the *San Francisco Chronicle* reported about one surprise appearance there in which, as a lark, the dancer "amus[ed] himself and amaz[ed] the customers by putting on a wig and female dress and popping up in the last show."

Mei Ling was not the first performer of Chinese heritage to appear as a female impersonator in San Francisco. Some fifty years earlier, Ah Ming (1828?–1892) dazzled theatergoers at the Washington Street Theater, where he earned $6,000 a year, a fabulous amount in those days. He was, wrote the *San Francisco Call*, "perfection in his special line, which was peculiar and a difficult character to assume…the coy manners and deportment of the Chinese girl of the period."

Not all his contemporaries were as beloved. According to the *Call*, "There is a Chinese female impersonator named Me Chung Chen, whom the theater-goers of little China have no use for. They claim he is a bad actor and ought not to be on the stage." During his appearance at the Chinese Theater on Jackson Street in 1903, "a serious riot occurred," with "eggs and rotten vegetables of all descriptions" being "hurled at the actors by an infuriated mob of motley Celestials."

Others fared much better. When Lou Yoke appeared at the San Francisco Hippodrome in 1916, the "Chinese female impersonator caused much admiration and merriment with his act." So did Roy Chan, a "native-born Chinese female impersonator with [a] cultivated soprano voice." Known as "the Chinese Nightingale," he performed at the Knights of Columbus Hall in 1922 with other entertainers for a charity fundraising event. Sadly, almost nothing else is known about either man.

Li-Kar (?–?) may or may not have been Chinese, although many believed he was; others thought his heritage was Indonesian. According to a brief biography that appeared in a Finocchio's souvenir program of the late 1940s or early 1950s, which he probably wrote himself, he trained as a commercial artist at Otis Art Institute and at Chouinard Art Institute, both in Los Angeles. He then enrolled in the Art Institute of Chicago. Still a student, he "became a free lance artist for two of Chicago's largest newspaper advertising concerns."

Li-Kar first appeared at Finocchio's in 1938. He was billed last of nine performers as Lee Carr, but his star was rising. Less than two years later, now as Li-Kar, he headlined at Club El Rio in El Cerrito. "East Bay Gets a New Sensation!!!" heralded the advertisement in the August 8, 1940 *Chronicle*, describing him as "America's Foremost Female Impersonator and Famed Interpretive Dancer. (S)he's Beautiful! (S)he's Terrific!"

Li-Kar specialized in "dances" of "the Far East." He also became known for creating more gowns for female impersonators than any designer in America. *Photograph by Theatrical Chicago.*

As both Lee Carr and Li-Kar, he continued at Finocchio's for almost three decades. Onstage he was a performer "specializing in dances of the Far East." In 1943, the *Examiner* described him as "one of the finest female impersonating dancers in the country." Within a few years, billed as the "Famed East Indies Dance Impressionist," he toured the country in "his own authentic dance creations from the world's concert stages."

In addition to his other contributions, Li-Kar did the artwork for many of Finocchio's souvenir programs, including one drawing where he included himself (*lower left corner*). Finocchio's souvenir program, circa 1949. *Author's collection.*

He also was making a name for himself as a costume designer. In 1940, *Chronicle* columnist Herb Caen wrote, "Gertrude Lawrence isn't one to forget a pal. Among her guests at the Palace Tuesday night…was Lee Carr, a boy who works up at Finocchio's. Last year, you see, Miss Lawrence admired a dress Lee wore in a show, so, because he had made it himself, he busily cut and stitched a copy for the star." Tallulah Bankhead also was an admirer.

Eventually, the fashions Li-Kar created became one more reason to see the show at Finocchio's. His "costumes are truly exquisite," the *Chronicle* informed its readers in 1941. As late as 1958, the paper, always a fan, noted, "The style-conscious will be interested in the beautiful costumes worn in Finocchio's lavish new revue," designed by Lee Carr. In 1965, the *Examiner* reported that "Li-Kar holds the record for having created more new ideas in gowns for female impersonators than any designer in America."

CHAPTER 19

THE BLACK SHEEP IN THE BLUE BOOK

San Francisco during the socially and sexually conformist 1950s. A middle-aged man taken into custody, charged with wearing a "woman's hairdo" and "flamboyant clothing" in public. It is a mundane police action, enforcing an ordinance passed in 1863 that made it a criminal act for anyone to appear on a public street in the city wearing "dress not belonging to his or her sex." This time, however, the charges were quickly dismissed because of the man's wealth and ancestry.

The man put under arrest was John Cabell Breckinridge III (1903–1996), whose paternal great-grandfather and namesake was vice president of the United States during the administration of James Buchanan (and also received the second-highest number of electoral votes for president in 1860, losing to Abraham Lincoln) and whose maternal great-grandfather, Lloyd Tevis, was a founder and president of Wells Fargo Bank from 1872 to 1892. "Bunny" to his friends, he was born in San Francisco in 1903 but grew up in Paris, surrounded by luxury.

After studying at Eton and Oxford University, Breckinridge returned to Paris, appearing in drag and burlesque revues as Jacques Solange for six years. In 1927, he married Roselle du Val de Dampierre, the daughter of a French noble; they were divorced two years later but not before having a daughter, named Solange, who later wed the Comte de Bruchard, giving Bunny two grandchildren.

Following his divorce, Breckenridge moved to San Francisco, where he intended to live a private life, as quietly and unassumingly as any

Bunny Breckenridge's 1922 passport photo showed him as the unflamboyant upper-class college student he was then. *Passport Applications, General Records of the Department of State, National Archives.*

Breckenridge made his only onscreen appearance as "the Ruler" in Ed Wood's notorious *Plan 9 from Outer Space*, often described as the worst film ever made. *Screen capture.*

openly gay man known for his flamboyant appearance, fondness for costume jewelry, drag performance and outrageous comments. Gore Vidal, who later took Bunny's last name for a famous title character, described him as a "feathered friend" and a "famous queen." (He also loaned his nickname to the foppish brother "Bunny" Wigglesworth in the film *Zorro, the Gay Blade.*)

In an era when homosexuality was illegal in every state, Bunny refused to be closeted, as fabulous as his closets were. He made headlines in 1954 when he announced plans to undergo sex reassignment surgery, an effort that his granddaughter supported. Reporters filed stories about "the He-She Millionaire," cataloged his "pinkie rings" and other "feminine accoutrements" for their readers and even described his home, with its "pale blue frills and flounces" and a bedroom where "pink and yellow bunnies nestle in… the bed."

An article in the *Los Angeles Mirror* was typical. Under the headline "Well-Known Visitor Flies in Fluttering," the newspaper reported that Breckinridge arrived in the city "wearing a pink ribbon in his hat, women's shoes, and a quart of perfume." He was delayed leaving the plane because "he had paused to dab some 'My Sin' perfume behind his ears." Bunny embraced the notoriety, but for numerous reasons, the operation for which he traveled there never took place.

In 1956, Breckinridge made his film debut in Ed Wood's *Plan 9 from Outer Space*, one of the most thoroughly analyzed motion pictures produced in Hollywood between *Citizen Kane* and *The Godfather.* With less than five minutes of screen time, he makes a memorable, lasting impression, displaying more ham than a state fair. Wood offered him a part in his next film, *The Dead Never Die*, but the project was not completed.

Bunny apparently knew everyone. His home in San Francisco was filled with photographs of the many celebrities he met and knew, including Princess Margaret, Noël Coward, Elvis Presley, Ed Sullivan, J. Edgar Hoover—of all people—and closeted Hollywood stars. None of them helped him in 1959, however, when he was convicted on ten counts of "sex perversion" for going to Las Vegas with two underage boys.

Bunny faced two possibilities at his sentencing. Because all homosexual relations were criminal acts, he might spend time in a state prison. Homosexuality itself, however, was a recognized mental illness, so he was sent instead to the state hospital for the criminally insane in Atascadero, California. Over the years, thousands of gay men received "medical cures" for their "condition" there, including electroshock treatments, aversion therapy, castration, hormone injection and "ice pick" lobotomies; all were legal, and no patient consent was necessary. His stay lasted a year.

Bunny survived both the scandal and his "rehabilitation." He turned to acting onstage, appearing in small, local theater productions into the 1960s. He died in 1996, at ninety-three years old. "I was a little bit wild when I was young, darling, but I lived my life grandly," he said. It may have been his only understatement.

Breckenridge was not the only San Franciscan with famous political forebears. Chester Alan Arthur III (1901–1972), known to everyone as Gavin, was the grandson and namesake of the twenty-first president of the United States. Notable as both a sexologist and an astrologer, he published *The Circle of Sex* in 1962, in which he explained that sexuality was a circle with twelve orientations, each corresponding to a sign of the zodiac.

Whether they believed he was a creative spirit, a colorful nonconformist or a kooky eccentric, whoever met him thought Arthur was memorable, a true "only in San Francisco" personality. Openly bisexual, he married three times but also was a key link in what Allen Ginsberg termed "the Gay Succession" from Walt Whitman to the present: "Walt Whitman

Married three times, commune founder, teacher, professional astrologer, sexologist and early gay rights activist Gavin Arthur often referred to himself as a "pre-hippie hippie." *Library of Congress.*

After Arthur divined its date, "The Gathering of the Tribes for a Human Be-In" received extensive public notice, including the cover of the January 1967 *San Francisco Oracle*, which chronicled the city's counterculture. *Wikimedia Commons.*

slept with Edward Carpenter who slept with Gavin Arthur who slept with Dean Moriarty who slept with Allen Ginsberg who slept with…"

A lifelong activist, Arthur was deeply involved with both the Beat Generation and the early gay rights movement. He also became an influential leader of the Haight-Ashbury counterculture, where he was part of the discussions about bringing together different groups in the Bay Area interested in expanding consciousness and increasing human potential, simply to experience "being" with each other. Using astrology, he set the date for the first "Human Be-In" for January 14, 1967, in Golden Gate Park.

Some thirty thousand celebrants attended. Many identified as hippies. They heard Ginsberg, Timothy Leary—who famously told them to "turn on, tune in, drop out"—Lenore Kandel, Gary Snyder and others speak about some of the basic tenets of the counterculture: personal empowerment, communal living, higher consciousness (achievable with the help of psychedelic drugs) and radical political awareness. Many simply enjoyed the day's "good vibrations" and "groovy sounds."

The event made the city's hippie scene world famous and led first to the "Easter Vacation Onslaught" and then to the transformative "Summer of Love." Young middle-class Americans from all over the country tripped to San Francisco, with or without a flower in their hair, leaving the comfort of their parents' homes or the conforming drabness of their dormitories for a Neverland where "there would be free love, free pot, free food and a free place to sleep."

Once in San Francisco, they traded in their button-down shirts and sorority sweaters for tie-dyed tees and fringed jackets. Khaki pants gave way to frayed bell-bottoms, and granny dresses replaced pleated skirts. In their rebellion against conformity, everyone wore beads. Haight-Ashbury quickly became both a mecca and a tourist attraction.

Among the head shops and psychedelic clothing stores of a neighborhood that embraced self-discovery, personal freedom, an "if it feels good, do it" attitude, sexual liberation and free love, the newly arrived found an established, vibrant LGBTQ+ community. It flourished even before the Summer of Love, at least back into the 1950s, and had created a lively main street for itself.

The year 1967 brought both setbacks and hope for the LGBTQ+ community. First, on March 7, CBS broadcast *The Homosexuals*. The first such television "documentary" seen by a national audience, it was described as "the single most destructive hour of antigay propaganda in our nation's history." Then California's State Department of Corrections announced an expanded work furlough program but stated homosexual prisoners would be excluded. Later, after Governor Ronald Reagan fired two of his aides for homosexual activity, he called homosexuality a "tragic illness" that "should remain illegal."

There was some good news, too, that year, when the Episcopal Diocese of California urged abolishing the laws regulating private sexual behavior. The cause was taken up by Willie Brown and John Burton of San Francisco, who in 1968 introduced a bill in the state legislature to do exactly that. Reintroduced each year for the next seven years, it finally passed and was signed into law by Governor Jerry Brown in 1975.

By the end of the Summer of Love, an estimated one hundred thousand people had journeyed to San Francisco, hoping to join, or at least behold, the city's counterculture. On October 6, the Diggers, a neighborhood group of activists and performers, held a funeral service for "Hippie, devoted son of Mass Media," to indicate that the tremendous cultural experiment that was the Haight-Ashbury had ended. It had, they felt, been co-opted, sanitized and commercialized out of existence.

LGBTQ+ culture and community, however, survived the invasion. Arthur died in 1972, but both he and Bunny surely would have been gladdened by how they endured in the Haight for another decade and now prosper throughout San Francisco.

CHAPTER 20

MADELINE GLEASON AND THE POETRY OF SAN FRANCISCO

Across her long creative career, Madeline Gleason (1903–1979) was a motivating influence and major champion of new poets and poetry of the Bay Area. Born in Fargo, North Dakota, she lived for a time in Portland, Oregon, then moved to San Francisco, where she worked on a history of California for the Works Progress Administration Writers' Project. By the time her first book, titled simply *Poems*, was published in 1944, she was deeply enfolded into the local literary potpourri.

Gleason was especially close to the poet Robert Duncan (1919–1988). The same year she published *Poems*, his essay "The Homosexual in Society" appeared in Dwight Macdonald's journal *Politics*. During an era when homosexuality was diagnosed as a mental disorder, Duncan argued simply that "a man's sexuality is a natural factor in a biological economy larger and deeper than his own human will." A pioneering document of gay liberation, it influenced lesbian and gay rights groups from the homophile '50s until the activist '70s and '80s.

Duncan had studied at the University of California, Berkeley, during the 1930s but dropped out in 1938. He returned to the campus in 1945, where he met two aspiring gay poets, Jack Spicer (1925–1965) and Robin Blaser (1925–2009), who would later edit *The Collected Works of Jack Spicer*, published in 1975. The three men shared so many avant-garde ideas about what poetry should be that they became a new literary movement, soon known as the Berkeley Renaissance.

Gleason was an avid supporter of the Berkeley Renaissance poets— and many other local poets. To present them to a wider audience, she

Left: Madeline Gleason not only wrote well-loved poetry, but she also founded the San Francisco Poetry Guild, organized the first poetry festival in the United States and often gave public readings with her colleagues. *Author's collection.*

Right: Muriel Rukeyser's poetry focused on equality, feminism, social justice and our shared humanity. In "Speed of Darkness" (2006), she wrote, "The Universe is made of stories, not of atoms." *Photograph by Nancy Naumberg, 1937. Escamandro.*

organized San Francisco's Festival of Modern Poetry in 1947, the first public celebration of poetry in the United States. Over two evenings at the Lucien Labaudt Gallery on Gough Street, twelve Bay Area poets read from their work, sometimes accompanied by music. For many of the participants, it was their first important recognition.

Because of Gleason's festival, San Francisco acquired a reputation as a major center of modern, experimental American poetry. In addition to Spicer, Blaser and Duncan, poet and activist Muriel Rukeyser (1913–1980), not yet out, was there, as well as poet and filmmaker James Broughton (1913–1999), who later became a member of the Radical Faeries and then Sister Sermonetta of the Sisters of Perpetual Indulgence.

The festival was a tremendous success. Not only aspiring poets but also painters, authors and playwrights from all over the country began moving to the city. The Berkeley Renaissance metamorphosed into the broader San Francisco Renaissance and then the Beat Generation of the 1950s.

None of the three movements was ever a rigid aesthetic or literary clique. They were loose associations of overlapping creative communities, made up of innovating minds who came to San Francisco looking for, and writing about, bohemian life in a world that was becoming increasingly conventional, conformist and intellectually repressive. The LGBTQ+ poets, however, often wrote of their loves and lives, ideals and realities denied and rejected by the mainstream culture.

Gleason continued to be influential within each new movement, however. In 1952, Duncan, the artist Jess Collins (1923–2004)—his loving and creative partner for thirty-seven years—and the painter Harry Jacobus (1927–) opened the King Ubu Gallery for alternative art in what had been an auto repair shop on Fillmore Street in San Francisco. Two years later, Spicer took over the space, renaming it the Six Gallery.

In 1955, five young poets, including Allen Ginsberg (1926–1997), until then mostly unknown beyond a close community of friends and writers, gathered at the Six Gallery to present selections from their latest works, some still in progress. The evening was transformational.

Ginsberg read "Howl," considered by many to be the greatest poem of his generation, one of the most important poems of the twentieth century and one of the greatest poems ever written by an American. Hugely influential and highly controversial, it confirmed to the world that San Francisco, always "an oasis of civilization in the California desert," was a true and vital center of counterculture originality.

Ginsberg, just thirty years old, published the poem in his first book, *Howl and Other Poems*, in 1956. In an era when American tastemakers applauded verse that described a doe as "a deer, a female deer," his impassioned, unsparing wail of anguish about "the best minds of my generation destroyed by madness," by conformity and by the norms of middle-class society, simply was not everybody's cup of tea ("a drink with jam and bread").

Almost immediately, the guardians of other people's propriety set upon the work and those who believed in it. First, customs officials impounded the poem's second printing when it arrived in San Francisco on March 25, 1957; only when the United States Attorney's Office declined to begin condemnation proceedings were the books released to their owners. Then, on June 3, two undercover police officers bought a copy and then arrested and jailed Shig Murao (1926–1999), manager of City Lights bookstore, for selling obscene literature. Poet Lawrence Ferlinghetti (1919–2021) was later arrested for publishing it.

One of the twentieth century's greatest and most influential poets, Allen Ginsberg remained always an outspoken champion of freedom of expression and sexual self-determination. *Photograph by Robert Pruzan. Robert Pruzan Papers (1998-36), GLBT Historical Society.*

At the subsequent obscenity trial, the defense argued simply that it was "not the poet but what he observes which is revealed as obscene." The court decided the work had "redeeming social importance," so the accused were pronounced not guilty. With findings by other courts that previously censored works could be sold in the United States, the ruling became a precedent for the United States Supreme Court when it established the criteria to determine if a publication can or cannot legitimately be subject to state regulation.

"Howl" became "the mantra of a generation" caught up in a society being shaped by the cookie cutters of modern times. Translated into more than twenty-two languages, it was among the most widely read poems of the twentieth century. Although most poets are known only to a few admirers, Ginsberg, like Walt Whitman before him, became familiar to millions who had not read any of his poetry.

Gleason's efforts to support and promote new poetry and its new ideas were confirmed with *The New American Poetry 1945–1960*, edited by Donald Allen (1912–2004). The first—now classic—anthology to include San Francisco Renaissance and Beat poets, it contained many of those Gleason championed: Blaser, Duncan, Spicer, Ginsberg and Broughton. Gleason's work was also there; she was one of only four women chosen.

In the late 1960s, Gleason and Mary Geer, who would be her life partner for more than twenty-five years, moved from North Beach to the Outer Mission. During the 1970s, she could be found on a Sunday afternoon at poetry readings at the Wild Side West, a lesbian bar in Bernal Heights. Her *Collected Poems*, with an introduction by Duncan, was published in 1999, twenty years after her death.

Making poetry so prominently and publicly the center of their lives, Gleason and her colleagues guided tremendous attention to their chosen art. They truly took poetry out of the ivory towers of academia and into the coffeehouses—and, occasionally, into the parks and onto the streets—making it available to anyone who wanted to listen to their words and hear their ideas. Because of her own work, and her work on behalf of poetry and the poets of San Francisco, Gleason remains a principal figure in the poetry of modern America.

PART IV

MOVERS, SHAKERS, PORNOGRAPHY MAKERS

HAL CALL: ACTIVIST FOR PROGRESS AND PORNOGRAPHY

Writing in *The Mayor of Castro Street*, the journalist and author Randy Shilts christened Hall Call San Francisco's "first permanent gay activist." One of the most important and controversial figures of the homophile movement of the 1950s and 1960s, he helped to shape its ideology and direction until the campaign for mainstream understanding and acceptance of lesbians and gays was superseded by the demand for direct action after Stonewall.

In an era of conformity and control, when too many people feared the very real consequences they faced for being openly lesbian or gay, Call was among the first to speak about homosexuality on radio and television, appearing as himself, using his real name. Born in Missouri in 1917 and educated as a journalist, he moved to San Francisco in 1952 after being acquitted of "lewd conduct" in Chicago.

He arrived at a difficult time for homosexuals in the United States. Two years earlier, in June 1950, the Senate began to investigate their employment by the government. The results were not encouraging. The Senate's report, titled *Employment of Homosexuals and Other Sex Perverts in Government*, concluded that homosexuals "constitute security risks" to the nation because "those who engage in overt acts of perversion lack the emotional stability of normal persons."

Homosexuality had long been illegal in the United States, but now gay men and women were being labeled both as undesirable employees and as threats to society—not for anything they did but for who they were.

The Senate's findings were bolstered in 1952, the year Call arrived in San Francisco, when the *American Psychiatric Association* classified homosexuality as a "sexual deviation" within the larger "sociopathic personality disturbance" category of personality disorders. Once viewed only as sinful and then as a crime, homosexuality was now codified by scientists as a mental illness.

The next year, on April 27, 1953, President Dwight Eisenhower signed Executive Order 10450, which declared homosexuals to be security risks and prohibited them, as well as alcoholics and neurotics, from working for the federal government; state and local governments approved similar restrictions, making sexual orientation the sole reason needed to fire an employee. Understandably, the changes drove people deep into their closets, not out into the streets.

The Mattachine Society, which held its first meeting in Los Angeles in November 1950, was the only gay rights organization to exist then. It was deeply divided about how to counter the assaults. Not only had its original leaders become hugely controversial because of their affiliations with the Communist Party, but two different views about how to move forward had also emerged among its members.

Some saw homosexuals as a minority group that needed to organize and press for its rights. Others believed that equality would come only by assimilating "as men and women whose homosexuality is irrelevant to our ideals, our principles, our hopes and aspirations." They wanted to educate the public that "our only difference is an unimportant one to the heterosexual society, unless we make it one."

After a bitter internal struggle that led to the resignation of the original leadership, Call became president of the society. Arguing that "the sex variant is no different from anyone else except in the object of his sexual expression," the group turned from considering any activism to favoring research and education. Its goal was sexual freedom through social understanding and acceptance, not political advocacy.

Call agreed. He believed that knowledge and influence would change minds; challenge and protest would only "foment an ignorant, fear-inspired anti-homosexual campaign." In 1954, he and associate Donald Lucas (1926–1998) founded Pan-Graphic Press to publish books, both fiction and nonfiction, that presented homosexuality objectively and explained it accurately. The press remained a successful business for years. It also printed the *Mattachine Review*, which Call edited, early issues of the *Ladder* for the Daughters of Bilitis and other homophile literature.

Hal Call, who received a Purple Heart after being wounded in the Pacific during World War II, became president of the Mattachine Society in 1953. *Courtesy of ONE Archives at the USC Libraries.*

As one of the first Americans to proclaim his "sexual deviation" publicly, Call began working with social scientists, local attorneys, journalists, community leaders and other professionals to help them better understand—and, hopefully, enable the public to better understand—what homosexuality "was all about." Many homophiles wanted to downplay their "sexual expression," but he was determined to educate the sexually uninformed by being open about it.

"Homosexualism," he told listeners to a 1958 radio program on KPFA, "is just one of the things that exists in nature. It always has been with us, as far as we know, and always will be as far as we expect. It seems that no laws, no attitudes of any culture…have ever been able to stamp it out or even essentially curb it." His goal was to "educate the public" about difference, so difference "will no longer be of any significance."

On September 11, 1961, Call appeared in *The Rejected*, the first documentary about gay men—nothing about lesbians was included—shown on American television. Produced by KQED in San Francisco, it examined "who are the gay ones, how did they become gay, how do they live in a heterosexual society, what treatment is there by medicine or psychotherapy, how are they treated by society, and how would they like to be treated?" Call presented the homophile viewpoint.

Many in the community were satisfied with how Call described them as ordinary citizens, but not everyone was pleased. A newer generation of activists thought the program was pandering. They believed that gays should be themselves, without apology or accommodation to the conceptions of mainstream society. Direct political action, not supplication, was the way to equality. It became the way of the future.

The Mattachine Society had entered a period of decline by the mid-1960s, but for many, Call remained the face of the "sexual variant." In 1964, he contributed to a *Life* magazine article that sought to explain "homosexuality—and the problem it poses." The same year, he was interviewed for *The Homosexual*, the first network documentary to discuss

mattachine
REVIEW

7TH ANNUAL CONVENTION   AUGUST 1960   50¢

September 1-5, 1960

San Francisco, Calif.

RECEIVED
AUG 31 1960

Theme:

"Let's Change Our
Outmoded Sex Laws"

(See Back Cover; Program Inside)

The *Mattachine Review*, which Hal Call edited and published from 1955 until 1967, contained articles that explained "the true facts of the Mattachine Society and the place of the sex variant in the life of the community." *Author's collection.*

homosexuality. No sponsor was willing to buy advertising time on it. Both showed that after a decade of work, public perception had hardly changed.

By then, the *Mattachine Review* was being published only sporadically; the last issue appeared in 1967. There was some good news that year, however, when gays received the right to look at pictures of their choice. Five years earlier, the United States Supreme Court ruled that photographs of nude men were not obscene, but many jurisdictions still prosecuted those who sold them, arguing they were illegal to send through the mail. The post office even canceled stamps with a slogan urging people, "Report Obscene Mail to Your Postmaster."

The risks did not stop Lloyd Spinar and Conrad Germain. In 1963, they founded Directory Services Inc. (DSI) to publish material of interest to gay men. Their first magazine, *Butch*, debuted in 1965; within a year, it was selling an astounding fifty thousand copies per issue. By 1967, DSI, with fourteen full-time employees, was the largest gay-owned, gay-oriented business in the world.

Then the government stepped in. It charged Spinar and Germain with twenty-nine counts of producing, promoting and mailing prurient material. Anything designed to appeal to homosexuals, it argued, was obscene because "the average person does not tolerate homosexuality and considers homosexual behavior morbid and shameful." The two men faced up to 145 years in prison, but eventually, the United States District Court of Minnesota disagreed.

After a thirteen-day trial, the court ruled that while homosexuality may or may not be a perversion, the materials "were not obscene simply because they might be aimed at a homosexual audience." Whether or not they appealed to the "degenerate" interests of some individuals, even those considered deviant by others, they "did not exceed current national limits of tolerance," and they "were not utterly without redeeming social value." The men were innocent of all counts.

In conclusion, the court offered an unprecedented, then-startling observation. The "rights of minorities expressed individually in sexual groups or otherwise must be respected." Germain and Spinar gave a large portion of the credit for their victory to Call, something of a last hurrah for his homophile activism.

The decision was binding only in Minnesota, but it set a precedent for other cases and showed that old restrictions and attitudes were disappearing. If anyone had doubts, San Francisco's 1967 Summer of Love proved it positively. The event made the new counterculture, with its philosophy of free speech, social rebellion, sexual revolution and free love, a nationally recognized movement.

Call went on to found the Adonis Bookstore the same year, the first gay bookshop in the United States. It carried periodicals and books as well as explicitly adult material, no longer against the law; much of it was created by Grand Prix Photo Arts, which he founded in 1968. What became the Circle J, the first gay adult theater in San Francisco with a live erotic stage show, followed soon after; it finally closed in 2005.

Some were disappointed that the former leader of the homophile movement had become a "mere pornographer," but Call was unapologetic about all of it. "What's the use in battling for sexual freedom without having any?" he asked. He died in San Francisco on December 18, 2000. He was eighty-three.

CHAPTER 22

DEL AND PHYL: PIONEERS FOR LESBIAN DIGNITY AND HUMAN RIGHTS

Del Martin (1921–2008) and Phyllis Lyon (1924–2020), life partners of fifty-six years, were two of the most formative and formidable individuals in the struggle to secure human rights for lesbians. At a time when there were no precedents, no prototypes and no strategies, they articulated the goals and implemented the course of action for the first organization for lesbians in the United States. Two unique individuals, they were so united in life, love and work that their stories cannot be told separately.

Del and Phyl met while both were working for a trade journal in Seattle. They moved together to San Francisco in 1953, renting an apartment on Castro Street, long before it emerged as a gay neighborhood. "We didn't know any other gay people," Del said subsequently, but eventually, a couple of gay men who lived nearby introduced them to two other women. When one of them mentioned the idea of starting a social club for lesbians, Del and Phyl wanted to be involved.

In October 1955, when no one was allowed to say "pregnant" on television and homosexuality could not be presented on the silver screen, four lesbian couples from diverse backgrounds gathered in a San Francisco home to establish a new and very different organization they called the Daughters of Bilitis (DOB). Their hope was to create an alternative to bars, which were frequently raided by police, where women could gather privately and meet each other without fear of being harassed or arrested for being themselves.

Above: When they moved to San Francisco in the 1950s, Del Martin (*left*) and Phyllis Lyon first lived on Castro Street and later moved to their longtime home in the neighborhood. *Phyllis Lyon and Del Martin Papers (1993-13), GLBT Historical Society.*

Opposite: An early meeting of the Daughters of Bilitis in Sausalito included (*left to right*) Del, Josie, Jan, Marge, Bev Hickok and Phyl, circa 1959. *Photograph by Cecil Davis. Phyllis Lyon and Del Martin Papers (1993-13), GLBT Historical Society.*

They named their new group in honor of the supposed author of *The Songs of Bilitis*, a collection of erotic lesbian poetry first published in Paris in 1894. All of them knew Bilitis had actually never existed, but they believed the reference would be meaningful only to like-minded women, thereby protecting their privacy. They also thought the name "would sound like any other women's lodge.…If anyone asked us, we could always say we belong to a poetry club."

The women showed exceptional bravery creating an organization for lesbians in the 1950s. More than sixty years later, the DOB's purpose may seem modest, but as the historian Lillian Faderman wrote, "Its very

establishment in the midst of witch-hunts and police harassment was an act of courage, since members always had to fear that they were under attack, not because of what they did, but merely because of who they were."

From the beginning, many women hesitated to join the group or even attend its meetings, concerned about what would happen should their sexual orientation become public knowledge, and they would be "exposed as perverts." Even though the group met in private homes at first, directions to find them were vague. A greeter stood at the door, telling newcomers, "I'm _____. Who are you? You don't have to give me your real name, not even your real first name."

The concern for privacy, even anonymity, was well founded. One report in the FBI's thick file for the DOB stated the organization was subversive because "the purpose of [this group] is to accept the Lesbian homosexual into society." For the government during the 1950s, that alone gave it justification to beware of the DOB's doings. The group's achievements would have been remarkable in any time, but during an era when homosexuality was condemned by medical science, legal authority and social mores, they were exceptional.

Del became the DOB's first president, Phyl its first secretary. Leaders of the organization for most of its first decade, the two women came to more closely personify it than anyone else. Originally, they planned to have three events a month: a cordial gathering, a discussion group and a business meeting. Very quickly, however, as Martin later explained in an interview, the goals of the organization became "to encourage and support the Lesbian in her search for personal, interpersonal, social, economic, and vocational identity."

None of this had been attempted before, and no wonder. Sexual acts between two consenting adults of the same gender were illegal in every state, territory and protectorate. The federal government had officially banned employing gays and lesbians. Homophobia was rampant. Meeting in private was one thing, but publicly announcing your sexual orientation was something else entirely. To create an organization for lesbians when individuals could lose everything simply because of who they were—jobs, homes, friends, family—was a courageous, daring, even perilous decision.

Not only did the DOB go public, but it also went national when it began the *Ladder* in 1956, the country's first publication for lesbians, a visible and important expression of their existence in American society. Phyl was the first editor, Del the first assistant editor. It started as a newsletter, printed on a mimeograph machine and assembled by hand, but it quickly became a magazine. Copies of the inaugural issue were mailed to some 175 women. Eventually, that number grew to about 1,000, with astonishing, often life-changing, results.

A typical issue of the *Ladder* included news, essays, poetry, short stories, book reviews, letters from readers and information about recent DOB meetings. Occasionally, it devoted an entire issue to the findings of a survey or study conducted by the organization's own research committee, which presented some of the first objective information gathered about lesbians in the United States.

The *Ladder* was published continuously from 1956 until 1972, a remarkable achievement in itself. "For women who came across a copy in the early days," the historian Marcia Gallo has written, it "was a lifeline. It was a means of expressing and sharing otherwise private thoughts and feelings, of connecting across miles and disparate daily lives, of breaking through isolation and fear." For many, it was their only contact with the lesbian community, showing them that they were not alone in the world.

Both career women, Del and Phyl knew that lesbians, who usually had to work to support themselves, often faced job discrimination in a world where their gender could keep them from being hired or promoted and their sexual orientation could get them fired. They concentrated always on very real concerns—job training, employment security, family rights—both as women in an anti-female society and as homosexuals in an anti-gay world, even as they moved toward more identification with the emerging feminist movement.

After they had been together for fifty-five years, Del and Phyl became the first same-sex couple to be wed in a civil ceremony in San Francisco in 2004. *Mayor's Office of Neighborhood Services.*

Their work as innovators, mentors and activists never stopped. In 1964, the two women became founding members of the Council on Religion and the Homosexual in San Francisco, an organization created to educate the city's religious communities about gay and lesbian issues. The next year, expanding its outreach to include elected officials, the group sponsored a "candidate's night," where LGBTQ+ residents could discuss their issues with local politicians, the first time anyone running for office publicly recognized or sought "the gay vote."

More firsts followed. When Del and Phyl joined the National Organization of Women (NOW) in 1968, created two years earlier, they were the first lesbian couple to do so. In 1972, they published the landmark *Lesbian/Woman* to describe "the everyday life experience of the Lesbian: how she views herself as a person; how she deals with the problems she encounters in her various roles as woman, worker, friend, parent, child, citizen, wife, employer, welfare recipient, home owner and taxpayer; and how she views other people and the world around her."

Del became the first openly lesbian member of NOW's national board in 1973. In 1976, she authored *Battered Wives*, which many consider the founding text of the "battered women's movement." After being together for more than fifty years, in 2004, she and Phyl became the first same-sex couple issued a marriage license in San Francisco, although it was soon invalidated by the California Supreme Court; they were again the first same-sex couple married after the court reversed itself in 2008.

Their courageous, pioneering work became the bedrock on which later organizations built. Some of these organizations, sadly, have not always valued the immense contributions of those whose groundbreaking achievements made them possible. Not only did Del and Phyl help lesbians across the country better understand themselves and their potential, but they also created a larger lesbian sensibility, one that showed two women could live together openly, honestly and successfully as friends, colleagues, lovers, life partners and spouses.

CHAPTER 23

THE DRAG QUEEN WHO CHANGED SAN FRANCISCO

O n a fateful afternoon, when Hazel, the pianist at the Black Cat in San Francisco's North Beach, was playing arias from *Carmen*, one of the waiters began singing along in a strong tenor voice as he brought his customers their drinks. Soon, he was performing four times a night, singing camp versions of then-popular torch songs, telling stories, chatting with people in the audience, reading them the paper and commenting about reports of police harassment of the gay community, always wearing his signature high heels.

From such serendipity can the fates of peoples and nations be decided. Born in 1922, José Sarria had not planned to be either a performer or an activist. He wanted to be a teacher, but that ambition ended during a visit to the Oak Room of the St. Francis Hotel, possibly the only gay bar in San Francisco history whose manager did not know it was a gay bar. So instead, he became the drag queen who changed the city's LGBTQ+ community and politics forever.

An elegant and discreet gathering place "for men only," the Oak Room was advertised as having "an atmosphere designed for masculine comfort." It boasted wood-paneled walls, a hand-painted ceiling and a white marble floor, but the actual facility for masculine comfort was down the hall. One evening, on a visit there, José was arrested and then convicted and heavily fined on a morals charge. He knew that a teaching career now was impossible. He turned to entertaining professionally "because I needed something to do."

José Sarria was famous for his drag performances as Carmen, Tosca and Madama Butterfly, but he also appeared as Eliza Doolittle. *Photograph by Robert Pruzan. Robert Pruzan Papers (1998-36), GLBT Historical Society.*

José soon became known as "the Nightingale of Montgomery Street." The arias from *Carmen* evolved into a Sunday afternoon extravaganza, one of his famous series of parody operas. *Madama Butterfly* was the first, but he also lampooned many others, including *Aida, Tosca* and even *My Fair Lady*. Rewritten for a gay audience, the operas highlighted some of the serious issues of discrimination and harassment gay men faced. Carmen, for example, now scrambled through the brambles of Union Square, not Seville, to avoid being arrested for cruising.

Overcapacity crowds adored these performances, even when José had in mind giving them more than a good laugh. At a time when the "experts" were telling them—and they believed—that they were mentally ill perverts, he wanted them to be proud of who they were and to stand up for their rights. He also shared some advice. "If you get tapped on the shoulder by a big blue star," his Carmen told them, "say, 'I'm not guilty and I want a trial by jury.'"

To forge a sense of both pride and community among the people in his audience, José had them stand up at the end of his performances, hold hands and sing the lyrics he shared in an interview with J.D. Doyle for *Queer Musical Heritage* in 2012:

> *God save us nelly queens,*
> *God save us nelly queens,*
> *God save us queens, and lesbians, too.*
> *From every mountain high*
> *Long may we live and thrive,*
> *God save us nelly queens,*
> *God save us queens.*

"I sang the song as a kind of anthem, to get them realizing that we had to work together," he told Michael Gorman. "We could change the laws if we weren't always hiding." For future activist George Mendenhall, and many others, Sarria's message to be proud of who you are was "the beginning of my awareness of my rights as a gay person."

In 1961, out and proud, José became a candidate for the city's board of supervisors. He had no problem raising the twenty-five-dollar filing fee, but getting twenty-five signatures for his nominating petition was difficult. "Nobody wanted to sign any paper helping or saying that they were going to back a homosexual," he remembered. He finally found either some "very bold queens" or some "closet queens who [I] had a little dirt on"—the story varied over time—and he was off and running.

Although he lost the election, José won some six thousand votes, confirming his claim that LGBTQ+ communities would come together for someone willing to fight for them. He also showed that they had enough votes to swing an election to one candidate or cause or another in a close contest. He was the first openly gay man to run for public office anywhere, and his candidacy changed local politics forever. "From that day, at every election, the politicians have talked to us."

As the journalist and historian Randy Shilts described it, on Halloween, the chief of police himself drove Sarria "to the center of North Beach... opening the car door politely for the elegantly gowned drag queen and giving the traditional send-off for the night's activities. 'This is your night—you run it.' For that one night, the police let homosexuals roam the city freely, even if they wore dresses....But when the hours shifted from October 31 to November 1, the iron fist of Lilly Law would fall again."

My Platform is Completely and Eloquently Engraved for All Time on the Facade of San Francisco's New **HALL OF JUSTICE** .TO THE FAITHFUL AND IMPARTIAL ENFORCEMENT OF THE LAWS ★ WITH EQUAL AND EXACT JUSTICE TO ALL ★ OF WHATEVER STATE OR PERSUASION ★ THIS BUILDING IS DEDICATED BY THE PEOPLE OF THE CITY AND COUNTY OF SAN FRANCISCO

JOSÉ JULIO SARRIA, Candidate for Supervisor
City and County of San Francisco
November 7, 1961

As a candidate for the board of supervisors, Sarria used what was probably the only photograph of himself wearing a suit and tie for his campaign literature. *Author's collection.*

Like many other cities then, San Francisco had an ordinance on its books that made it illegal for men to dress as women in public, ostensibly to protect the naive or gullible from being misled or swindled for illicit or lustful purposes. The "intent to deceive" gave the police all the reason they needed to begin harassing and arresting tastefully costumed gays in the early hours of All Saints' Day as they left bars and parties on their way home.

José sought a solution. First, he researched the ordinance, thought about its specific wording and consulted with renowned attorney Melvin Belli, whose law offices were next door to the Black Cat. Then he made up tags for everyone to wear that stated, "I am a boy." Anybody stopped by the police could simply explain, "The law states it is unlawful to dress with an intent to deceive, but I am stating my gender plainly."

The police may not have liked it, but they understood their legal risk from arresting someone—even a gay man—who they knew was not guilty, especially with Belli, celebrated as "the King of Torts," involved. They did not stop harassing gays, however, or working with the state's Department of Alcoholic Beverage Control to close the city's gay bars. On Halloween 1963, after years of legal actions, they successfully revoked the Black Cat's liquor license, forcing it to close for good.

The year José ran for supervisor, he also cofounded the League for Civil Education, paying the startup costs for the new nonprofit himself. The

As Her Royal Majesty, Empress de San Francisco, José I the Widow Norton, Sarria remained active with the International Court System he founded until 2007. *Photograph by Robert Pruzan. Robert Pruzan Papers (1998-36), GLBT Historical Society.*

group survived for only two years, but the Society for Individual Rights, which followed it, lasted for almost two decades. Neither apologetic nor assimilationist, like some earlier homophile organizations, it opened a community center and sponsored social clubs, dances, candidates' nights and theatrical productions, including its annual Sirlebrity Capades, at which José sang everything from *Aida* to Edith Piaf.

In 1964, the recently formed Tavern Guild, the first LGBTQ+ business association in the United States, named José queen of its annual Beaux Arts Ball. Announcing that he was already a queen, he proclaimed himself Empress José Norton the First, in homage to San Franciscan Joshua Norton, who declared himself emperor of the United States and protector of Mexico in 1859. His first official appearance was a week later when he officiated at the local opening of the Ice Follies.

A year later, José founded the Imperial Court System, now one of the largest LGBTQ+ organizations in the world, with more than sixty-five chapters in North America. As Her Royal Majesty, Empress de San Francisco, José I the Widow Norton, he remained active in the organization until 2007, then abdicated in favor of his heir apparent. When he died six years later, more than one thousand mourners attended his imperial drag-themed funeral at Grace Cathedral on Nob Hill, where he once had picketed.

Time proved that José was right. Affirming LGBTQ+ identity, inspiring pride, creating community, increasing visibility and building political strength were the means to effect change. Throughout his life as a performer and an activist, he made two truths clear to his sisters and brothers. The first: "There's nothing wrong with being gay—the crime is getting caught," he said consistently, until the anti-sex laws finally were repealed. The second, "United we stand, divided they catch us one by one," carved on his tombstone, remains counsel to remember always.

CHAPTER 24

VACAVILLE 1956:
CALIFORNIA'S FIRST GAY RIGHTS PROTEST

T he first known protest in California by a group of gay men against their mistreatment because they were homosexual, authorities said later, really began with a simple misunderstanding. Only fifty miles northeast of San Francisco, on September 9, 1956, a correctional officer told some forty-five residents gathered in the second-floor dayroom of Vacaville State Hospital's K Wing—"the section designated for homosexuals"—that he was going to pick up their "hobby work."

According to a report filed the next day, the "homosexuals in K Wing," contrary to stated rules, had "accumulated handicraft articles, clippings, pictures and other things with which they have decorated their rooms." These now would be taken from them, and the men would be forbidden from displaying "in their housing quarters" any "items of handicraft, such as doilies, picture frames, etc."

When the officer on duty explained he was going "to enforce the regulations," the men were not pleased. "Some of the inmates protested in no uncertain manner," he explained later. In addition to booing and calling him an "S.O.B. Bull," they went down to his office and knocked everything from his desk onto the floor.

To better understand the disturbance, staff agreed to interview anyone who wished to share his grievances. Beside losing their hobby privileges, inmates complained about "the minor harassments and frustrations" that came from "the restrictions necessarily imposed upon this particular housing unit," which created "an area of acute sensitivity to homosexual patients."

Even more serious, many also "regard[ed] their K Wing housing as a form of daily punishment due to their being homosexuals."

Sharing grievances did not end the enmity. Inmates continued to challenge their treatment as best they could. Some papered over their cell windows; others covered them with shoe polish or soap. Twice they removed furniture from the wing's dayroom, taking it to their ward. Finally, on September 23, approximately twenty-five residents left the cafeteria and proceeded back to the unit unescorted, a serious violation of protocol.

That was enough protest for the administration, which now responded swiftly to the events it once characterized as minor. Staff identified eight men who were allegedly "constantly fomenting and agitating" an atmosphere of "complete and general disrespect and disregard of authority in Wing K." Three were moved to Wing S and placed in segregation. Five, "determined not [to] be psychotic" but who "have not responded to treatment provided," were transferred to Folsom Prison.

The report did not name the treatment, but the medical staff had numerous options. They included counseling, castration, electric shock therapy, massive injections of male hormones, mood-altering medicines, aversion therapy and psychosurgery, popularly known as leucotomy or prefrontal lobotomy. Inmates were under the care of court-appointed medical professionals, and the "appropriate" therapy was chosen by an attending physician. Patients had no legal say in their treatment.

The worst of times for homosexuals in California began in 1949, when the state established procedures that allowed indefinite detention of "sexual psychopaths." State trial judges now had the flexibility to designate gay men charged with sodomy or oral copulation—both illegal—either as criminals to be punished or as mentally ill personalities to be "healed." Instead of being sentenced to prison for five to ten years, they now could be incarcerated in a psychiatric prison hospital "until cured," potentially for the rest of their lives.

Leucotomy, the most notorious "cure," was developed by the Portuguese neurologist António Egas Moniz, who won a Nobel Prize in Medicine for it in 1949. The physician credited with popularizing it in the United States was Walter Freeman. His streamlined version of the operation, known as a transorbital or "ice pick" lobotomy, took ten minutes or less to complete; patients were made unconscious with electroconvulsive shock. It could be done anywhere, including mental hospitals that had no operating rooms or even surgeons on staff.

Freeman performed as many as five thousand lobotomies during his career, up to 40 percent of them on homosexuals; some five hundred individuals died because of the treatment. In 1971, he announced that he himself had "severed the frontal lobes" of homosexual inmates at California's Atascadero State Hospital, the most notorious mental health care facility in the state. The next year, the public learned that at least three inmates had undergone the procedure at Vacaville.

Help for the helpless came soon after. In 1973, the American Psychiatric Association removed homosexuality from its list of mental disorders. Then California decriminalized same-sex intimacy. No longer deemed mentally ill and no longer being convicted for "homosexual behavior," gay men stopped being sent to mental hospitals because of whom they chose to love. New drugs eventually ended lobotomy as a "cure" for unacceptable and antisocial behavior in California, although the state did not ban so-called gay aversion therapy until 2012.

Vacaville may have been the site of the first protest in California by gay men against their treatment for being members of a sexual minority, but it was not the last. In May 1959, transgender women and drag queens pelted police with donuts and coffee cups at Cooper Do-nuts in Los Angeles when, once again, they were hassled there by officers. In August 1966, transgender women and gay men stood up for their rights at Gene Compton's Cafeteria in San Francisco. Other incidents followed, including one at the Stonewall Inn in New York, which ignited a revolution.

Quotations are from documents in "Projects & Programs—Incidents—C. M. F., Vacaville 1951–59, Corrections-Correctional Program Services, 1951–59," Correctional Program Services Records, Department of Corrections, California State Archives, Sacramento.

CHAPTER 25

RIKKI STREICHER:
CHAMPION OF FREEDOMS AND RIGHTS

L egendary entrepreneur, community business leader and passionate sports activist, Elizabeth "Rikki" Streicher (1926–1994) was a leader in the movement to gain human rights for LGBTQ+ people in San Francisco. As the owner of three bars for women, she recognized early on that the city's bar-based communities, mostly overlooked by the assimilationist homophile organizations of the time, could become informed local voters and organize for political action to overturn the legalized discrimination against them and their ways of life.

Streicher opened Maud's, her first bar, at 937 Cole in 1966. The former site of the Study, also a bar, it was called Maud's Study for a while, "the name being a sort of lesbian code for its patrons," writes Jane Chamberlin in *The Great and Notorious Saloons of San Francisco* (1982). If overheard in public, "women going to 'The Study' were women likely to be going to the library."

Maud's became a popular, then legendary watering hole in the Haight-Ashbury, a place where women could meet, find each other, discover community, gossip, hug. At the time it opened, California law forbade women from being bartenders in clubs they did not own, so the honor of pouring drinks in the early years went to men from nearby gay establishments. When it closed in 1989, it was the longest-surviving lesbian bar in the country.

From the start, Maud's was home base for Streicher's political activism. The 1974 edition of *Girl's Guide* noted that it was "very Gay Lib oriented," its walls filled with public notices for events and benefits for the women's community, gay and straight. Even so, the focus at Maud's, according to

In the 1940s, when Rikki Streicher (*left*) and friends had their photograph taken at the Claremont Hotel in Oakland, a butch-femme dichotomy was commonly used to categorize lesbians and define their relationships. *Wide Open Town Records (2003-05), GLBT Historical Society.*

the *Advocate Guide* (1982), was on playing pool and listening or dancing to music on the jukebox.

Streicher believed early on in bar culture. She joined the Tavern Guild and served on its board of directors. Formed in 1962 in response to ongoing raids by police of lesbian and gay establishments, it was the first LGBTQ+ business association in the United States. It defended the rights of its members, their employees and their patrons; retained legal assistance for anyone arrested near a gay or lesbian bar; and raised money for important work. It also began inviting politicians to its meetings. Recognizing the possibilities, many attended.

The year Streicher opened Maud's was a momentous one for the city's expanding LGBTQ+ community. Although Fin Alley at 834 Irving, with its go-go girls on the bar, closed in 1966, two other taverns for women opened. The Parkwood Lounge at 2001 Irving had limited success, but Peg's Place at 4737 Geary lasted until 1988. Fin's owner, Charlene Scott, launched Highlander the next year, then Scott's Pit in 1970, which became "the closest thing to a lesbian leather bar in San Francisco."

In addition, 1966 saw new bars for men open in four of the city's LGBTQ+ neighborhoods: the Lucky Club at 1801 Haight, Off the Levee at 527 Bryant near the Embarcadero, the Tower Lounge at 1488 Pine in Polk Gulch and both FeBe's at 1501 Folsom and the Stud at 1535 Folsom, contributing to what was well on the way to becoming leather's "Miracle Mile."

Two of the city's earliest public demonstrations challenging the bigotry people in the LGBTQ+ community faced in their daily lives also occurred in 1966. On Armed Forces Day, May 21, gay men rallied on the steps of the Federal Building in San Francisco's Civic Center to protest their exclusion from the military, this at a time when the draft was still in force and the war in Vietnam was rapidly escalating.

The following August, the Compton's Cafeteria in the Tenderloin became a battleground between LGBTQ+ people and police when a group of customers, many of whom were drag queens and trans women, fought back against the men in blue, who constantly and often violently harassed them. Not only was it a bumpy night, but it was also the first time LGBTQ+ San Franciscans forcibly resisted their oppression.

Streicher opened Amelia's at 647 Valencia Street in 1978 (the building originally housed a mortuary). Advertising itself as a "woman's bar and disco," it also had a pool table but was, reported the *Advocate* in its 1981 *Gay Visitor's Guide*, "especially recommended if you love to dance." The second floor, which featured a stage, was often used for community events and benefits.

The bar was named for pioneer aviator Amelia Earhart. Previous tenants in the space had not lasted long. The Gaslight, which opened there in 1972, survived for about a year; it featured drag shows, then gay melodramas, then nude go-go boys before being raided and shut in 1973. In 1977, it became the Gay 20's Speakeasy, which closed in 1978. Streicher's establishment retained its popularity for thirteen years, having its last night in 1991.

Olive Oil's Bar and Grill, Streicher's third establishment, opened at Pier 50 in 1982. The next year, when Queen Elizabeth and Prince Philip concluded their visit to San Francisco, Mary Ann Singleton, according to Armistead Maupin, writing in *Babycakes* (1984), watched their yacht, the *Britannia*, sail off toward the Golden Gate while sitting on a stool in the bar. Promoted as a lesbian drinkery, it also attracted many gay men.

Rikki was a passionate sports enthusiast, and she sponsored women's sports teams for bowling, volleyball, pool and basketball. Baseball, however, remained her favorite, an enthusiasm rewarded in 1976 when Maud's team won the first-place championship in the Bay Area Women's Softball League.

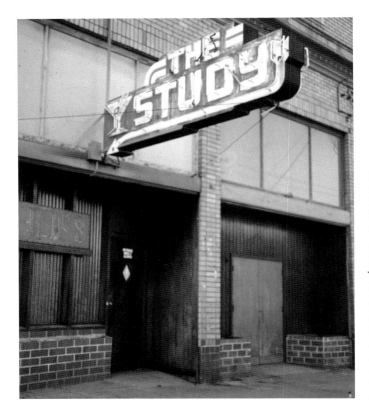

During the twenty-three years Maud's was open between 1966 and 1989, its patrons included singer Janis Joplin, activists Del Martin and Phyllis Lyon, poet Judy Grahn and feminist Sally Gearhart. *Photograph by Henri Leleu. Henri Leleu Papers (1997-13). GLBT Historical Society.*

Streicher helped to organize the Gay Games in San Francisco in 1982, then went on to cofound the Federation of Gay Games, its successor organization.

At the fourth annual games in New York in 1994, Streicher received the Dr. Tom Waddell Award for her contributions to gay athletics. Rikki Streicher Field, in the heart of the Castro, also recognizes her contributions to LGBTQ+ sports. In 2018, she was saluted with a plaque on the city's Rainbow Honor Walk as an "entrepreneur and sports advocate who brought San Francisco's bar based communities into the City's movement for LGBT rights."

CHAPTER 26

SISTERS OF BILITIS

P at "Dubby" Walker (1938–1999) had not heard of the Daughters of Bilitis (DOB) until Billye Talmadge, one of the organization's cofounders, visited Oakland's Orientation Center for the Blind in 1958. "She picked me out as gay," Walker remembered. "She started taking me to different things" and introduced her to many of the women involved in the organization. "There were parties, picnics, getting together to work on [the *Ladder*]," the group's monthly publication. Two years later, she became the first Black president of the San Francisco chapter.

The world of 1960 was very different from today. Homosexuality was illegal in all fifty states, including the two newest, admitted to the Union only the year before. By executive order of then-president Dwight Eisenhower, anyone working for the federal government discovered to be homosexual was fired immediately; no known gay men or lesbians could be hired, and they had no legal protections anywhere. In San Francisco, police often arrested people simply for touching someone of the same sex, claiming lewd conduct or worse.

"Dubby" had four strikes against her succeeding in that world. Black, female, blind and lesbian, she was fortunate in one way, at least: she had a sympathetic and supportive home life. "When I was eleven or twelve, my mother told me about gayness," she shared with an interviewer in 1988. "My mother had gay friends and my sister is also gay. At fourteen I realized I liked girls. I never felt bad about myself because of it."

Determined to live an independent life, Walker learned "how to use her other senses to 'see' her way." She refused a Seeing Eye dog. "They get all the credit," she said. She supported herself first with a telephone wake-up service and then by operating a convenience shop in the lobby of a downtown Berkeley office building. No disadvantage or disability, Del Martin wrote later, "stopped her from being an activist and making the world a better place for women, lesbians, African Americans, and the blind."

In 1964, Walker was one of five representatives of the DOB at a retreat in Mill Valley that hoped to establish "better understanding between homosexuals and organized religion." The result: the Council on Religion and the Homosexual (CHR), "the first group in the U.S. to use the word 'homosexual' in its name." While actively working to let gays and straights alike know that "Gay Is Good," it became an important source of legal and political support for San Francisco's LGBTQ+ communities.

Cleo Bonner (?–?), the first Black national leader of the Daughters and the first woman of color to lead a national LGBTQ+ organization, was also at the retreat. She had joined the San Francisco chapter of the DOB four years before, in 1960, when she was already in a committed relationship with a woman, raising a son and working at Pacific Bell, which some years later admitted that "we do not knowingly hire or retain…homosexuals." To protect herself and her family, she became known as Cleo Glenn.

Not only did Bonner almost immediately take on the job of circulation manager for the *Ladder*, but with her partner, she also ran the DOB's Book Service, at a time when "education of the variant" and "education of the public" were among the organization's most important goals. Women now could access information, literature, novels about lesbians that were "well-written and ending happily" and music—"the gayest songs on wax"—they dared not ask for and often could not find where they lived.

In June 1964, Bonner traveled to New York with Phyllis Lyon and Del Martin to attend the DOB's third national convention, themed "The Threshold of the Future." She had been elected to the organization's national governing board in 1961, appointed acting president two years later and elected president in 1964. Welcoming the delegates, she acknowledged, "We have our struggles and disappointments," although the convention itself was "quite a world-shaking event." She encouraged everyone to "go on a little longer, to help where we can and do what we can."

Bonner's term as national president ended in August 1966, two months after Ernestine Eckstein (1941–1992), vice president of the DOB's New York chapter, became one of two Black women to appear on the cover of the *Ladder*. Like Bonner, she dared not use her true last name, but unlike Bonner and many of her peers, she wanted to do more than "help where we can." She saw the value of protests and demonstrations and was willing to picket, very visibly, even in front of the White House.

Although only two years younger than Walker, Eckstein belonged to a new generation, one that believed public activism, not education and cooperation, was the best way to bring about society's acceptance of gay men and lesbians. As an undergraduate at Indiana University, Bloomington, she was involved in her local NAACP chapter. After moving to New York, she joined the Mattachine Society, the DOB and the Congress of Racial Equality, which "pioneered the use of nonviolent direct action in America's civil rights struggle."

Many in the homophile movement, for very real reasons, found visibility threatening, but for Eckstein, it was the key to securing their rights. "Homosexuals are invisible, except for the stereotypes," she told Kay Tobin and Barbara Gittings in a lengthy interview for the *Ladder*'s June 1966 issue, "and I feel homosexuals have to become visible and to assert themselves politically. Once homosexuals do this, society will start to give more and more."

THE LADDER
Adults Only .50
June 1966
A LESBIAN REVIEW

Featuring a photograph by Kay Tobin of Ernestine Eckstein on the cover, the *Ladder*'s June 1966 issue included a lengthy interview with Eckstein by Tobin and her partner, Barbara Gittings. *Author's collection.*

"The discrimination by the government in employment and military service, the laws used against homosexuals, the rejection by the churches" had to be confronted openly. "The homosexual has to call attention to the fact that he's been unjustly acted upon," she said. "A movement needs a certain number of courageous people, there's no getting around it. They have to come out on behalf of the cause and accept whatever consequences come." Eckstein certainly was among the first few, if not the first, to use the phrase "come out."

Where Walker and Bonner had ably implemented the DOB's original stated purpose of educating women, the public, researchers and legislators to effect change, Eckstein now heralded the future course of the LGBTQ+ civil rights movement. Demonstrations, she said, "are one of the very first steps toward changing society." She moved from New York to Northern California in the early 1970s, joined Black Women Organized for Action and continued her activism. She died in San Pablo, Contra Costa County, in 1992.

CHAPTER 27

THE TRIALS OF CHARLES CHRISTMAN

Shortly after closing time at the Stud on Saturday, December 12, 1970, between 100 and 150 last callers were leaving the bar when a patrol car with two police officers pulled up. Some patrons were still chatting with old friends; some were still hoping to make new ones; many were already walking to their cars. The officers, claiming the men were blocking traffic on Folsom Street, ordered them to disperse immediately.

Because people appeared to linger, the patrolmen called for backup. Two more squad cars, each with two officers, arrived within minutes. Then all six policemen strode into the crowd. During the confusion that followed, several individuals were arrested, primarily on charges of failing to disperse or interfering with law enforcement. One man, however, faced very serious charges: five felony counts of assaulting police officers with a deadly weapon.

Charles Christman, twenty-seven, an ecology student at San Francisco State, was driving away when the patrolmen ordered him to stop. According to one eyewitness, "Police began firing at the car" when "it tried unsuccessfully to get around a police car blocking the street." The driver, he added, was "shot as he tried to run off after his car was peppered" with bullets. Soon in custody, he was taken to San Francisco General Hospital, where physicians discovered he had bullet wounds in his back, elbow and ankle.

The *San Francisco Examiner* described the incident of the "Gay Bar Ruckus" the next day, explaining to readers, "'Gay' bars are frequented by male homosexuals." The paper reported that, according to the police, Christman

Police shot Charles Christman as he drove away from the Stud, described in *QQ Magazine*'s summer 1970 issue as "the turned-on, spaced out super groovy bar where heads meet." *Photograph by Henri Leleu. Henri Leleu Papers (1997-13). GLBT Historical Society.*

"tried to run down four officers," but missed. Then "he bowled over" a fifth officer, "who was slightly injured."

The details of the incident were disputed almost immediately. Was the crowd actually blocking traffic on Folsom Street? Did anyone jeer at the police, calling them "pigs"? Did the officers shout their own epithets at the bar's patrons? Did they beat people with their clubs? Was Christman trying to injure the police or simply trying to leave the area? Were Christman's actions deliberate or frantic? It would be left to the courts to decide.

Altercations between police, often working with the state's Alcoholic Beverage Control Board, and members of San Francisco's LGBTQ+ communities were nothing new. Bar raids, harassment, liquor license suspensions and entrapment, especially of gay men, had become increasingly frequent in the years after World War II, the era of America's "Lavender Scare." Citing vagrancy and lewd conduct laws, officers even stopped and questioned individuals walking alone in public.

The largest raid of a gay bar in San Francisco, although not the last, came on August 13, 1961, when police arrested eighty-nine men and fourteen women at the Tay-Bush. Eventually, two men were found guilty of lewd conduct. "We don't need people like you in California," the judge told them. "Go back to where you came from." The case against owner Robert Johnson was dismissed when he agreed to close his business.

In those earlier times, Christman might have been left to his legal burden and his fate. Not now. The strategy crystalized by Stonewall the year before was clearly understood by some of the city's leading LGBTQ+ organizations, who were already defending the community's civil rights: visibility, resistance, organization, protest. Fairly new themselves, these organizations included the Tavern Guild, formed in 1962, and the Council on Religion and the Homosexual (CHR) and the Society for Individual Rights (SIR), both founded in 1964.

The three organizations immediately came together to develop a legal defense and to provide financial assistance for those who had been arrested. Evander Smith, an attorney for the Tavern Guild who was well known among lesbians and gays, agreed to defend them in court. As chair of the SIR's legal committee, he had written *In Case of Arrest: The SIR Pocket Lawyer*, a pocket-size pamphlet of legal dos and don'ts published in 1965.

By 1970, SIR was the largest homophile organization in the country. Unlike earlier groups, which focused on educating their members and the public about homosexuality, its goals included publicly affirming gay and lesbian identity, building community, eliminating laws against same-sex intimacy between consenting adults, hosting political forums for candidates and elected officials, providing leisure activities and entertainment for the community and offering needed social services—including legal aid—to "gays in difficulties."

SIR had begun working with the police department as early as 1966, but Christman's ordeal threatened to destroy these efforts. On April 30, just before his second trial was to begin, SIR held a benefit dance at its Community Center at 83 Sixth Street for his legal defense fund. The event was intended not only "to help Charles Christman" but also "to demonstrate to the police department of this city that the wanton use of deadly force against members of our community will no longer be tolerated."

Not everyone in the community was sympathetic to Christman's plight. *California Scene*, a homophile entertainment magazine, thought "the recent altercation between the police and some gay hippie types outside The Stud was foreseeable." Describing it as a bar that attracted "gay hippies, straight hippies and student gays of confused mind and political persuasion," it stated that the incident "has little to do with the average guy doing a pub crawl along Folsom Street."

How wrong *California Scene* was. Not only had gay men been harassed leaving a public place, but they had also been threatened with violence. Testimony at Christman's trial showed an enormous lack of understanding about homosexuality on the part of many police officers, who needed "little to trigger selective or overreactive behavior" and "a hostile reaction"—a potential peril for any "average guy" doing "a pub crawl" in a gay area. Christman could have been killed.

When Christman's trial began in March 1971, some were surprised that homosexuality itself was not its focus, although Assistant District Attorney John Dwyer made sure the jury knew that the Stud was a gay bar. He also asked defense witnesses about their marriage status, intimating that because they were homosexual, their testimony was not credible. Whether or not his strategy worked, the trial ended in a hung jury, 10–2 for conviction.

The district attorney's office refiled the charges, but almost immediately after the new proceedings began the next month, a compromise settlement ended all litigation. The five felony indictments against Christman were dismissed when he agreed to plead guilty to two misdemeanor charges. For those, he then received a suspended jail sentence, a fine of $625 and three years' probation. His record was to be expunged at the end of the probationary period.

On May 19, SIR hosted a public meeting to discuss ideas for improving relations with the police. More than six hundred people attended, including representatives from virtually every "homosexual organization in the city." It would be another five years before same-sex intimacy between consenting adults became legal in California.

CHAPTER 28

WAKEFIELD POOLE: "NO MORE CLOSETS"

Wakefield Poole created the modern gay adult film in 1971 when he was living in New York. Made on a budget of $4,000, *Boys in the Sand* was the first feature-length XXX motion picture ever produced with an all-male cast and the first to present interracial male-male intimacy. It was the first to include on-screen credits for its cast and crew, although many used noms de porn. It was the first to reviewed by *Variety*, the entertainment industry's "journal of record," and the first to gain mainstream credibility.

Variety was a bit premature when it announced the film's popularity meant that "there are no more closets," but *Boys* helped to bring about the era of "porno chic," that brief period of open cultural acceptance of hardcore pornography. It also helped to change stereotypes of gay men by presenting its star, Casey Donovan (né Calvin Culver) as the clean-cut, all-American boy next door, although he certainly was less sexually reserved both on- and offscreen. Donovan became gay porn's first celebrity superstar.

"I wanted [to make] a film that gay people could look at and say, 'I don't mind being gay—it's beautiful to see those people do what they're doing,'" Poole said some years later. Whatever their motivation, gays, straight couples and women went to see the movie in record numbers; it made back its production costs in a single theater the day it opened. Unlike most gay adult films, which have a limited appeal of months or weeks, *Boys* is still in distribution after more than fifty years.

Poole directed two more adult films in New York before moving to San Francisco with his lover Peter Schneckenburger, who appeared in *Boys in the*

Sand as Peter Fisk; a friend from New York, Harvey Milk, helped them find their first apartment. In 1975, the couple opened Hot Flash of America at 2351 Market Street as "a totally gay-owned enterprise." It was located half a block from Seventeenth and Castro Streets. Poole "wanted to make sure it represented a truly complex view of the homosexual world."

The view was indeed complex but very much reflected a Greenwich Village/Castro Street/West Hollywood sensibility. On display and available for purchase, Poole wrote in his autobiography, were "antique French marble candy counters beneath Lalique mirrors, next to San Francisco street lamps, beside a wicker chair, covered with Mao silk pillows, alongside a rubber chicken." The inventory also included coffee mugs made to resemble a pair of cutoff Levi's, erotic cloisonne jewelry, sterling silver joint holders, novelty items that cost a dollar and original art costing thousands.

Living up to its motto—"Everything You Want but Nothing You Need!"— it was described by *California Hotline* as being "a super-creative store that is both an art gallery and a store with antiques and whatever—all distinctive." The *Advocate* thought so, too. "A walk into Hot Flash can brighten even the bluest spirit," it reported. "They raise the concept of gift shops almost to an art form."

All of this was a bit too much for the *San Francisco Bay Guardian*. Yes, Hot Flash was "easily the area's arbiter, incontestably Castro Street's pacesetter and benchmark, the apotheosis of what a gift shop can aspire to." Ultimately, however, "just like its mirrored bathroom, there's too much paradox going on here." Even "delineating what's sold here is irrelevant because it changes constantly. This change is its real product.…This place has rhythm, the measure of now, its fingers firmly counting the pulse of the public's pocket."

Whether Hot Flash set trends or followed them, it became a very popular destination. The inventory was redone every six weeks, previewed with an invitation-only reception. There was also a hair salon in the rear of the store, so customers could get prettified for their Saturday date in the back and then buy their beau a gift—anything from a T-shirt to an original work of art—in the front, all in one stop.

The Hot Flash T-shirt, emboldened with a logo that was modeled after Arm & Hammer's famous trademark, soon became an essential item in every Castro clone's wardrobe, which also included tennis shoes or boots, snug 501s, a flannel shirt for cooler days, a polo shirt for dressier occasions and a hooded jogging jacket (affectionately known as a "fag wrap") or bomber jacket (green or black). Unfortunately, the clones bought more T-shirts than antiques, making the business finally unprofitable. It closed in 1979.

Hot Flash of America, wrote *California Hotline*, was "a super-creative store that is both an art gallery and a store with antiques and whatever—all distinctive." *Photograph by James Armstrong. Author's collection.*

Just behind Hot Flash, facing Seventeenth Street, was the Beau Geste Cinema. It opened in May 1976 with a screening of *This Is the Army*, starring Ronald Reagan, but its life as a revival house did not last long. By October, it was showing gay adult films exclusively, the only XXX movie theater ever in the neighborhood. It became the East of Castro Club in 1979, its films now projected on the walls above the private booths on the first floor and the holed partitions in the balcony.

Clif Newman, who managed the new enterprise, also managed the XXX Nob Hill Cinema, which previously had been a jazz club. He and Poole were good friends, so perhaps it was inevitable that the Nob Hill became the location for *Take One* as well as its world premiere in 1977. Using documentary, performance art and observational cinema techniques, Poole presented a series of interviews with gay San Franciscans who discussed their lives and sexual fantasies before living them out in front of his camera.

In 1980, Poole moved back to New York, where he had been a dancer and choreographer on Broadway and television before making *Boys*. He directed five more XXX features and then left the adult industry in 1985 to become a trained chef. He next worked as manager of food services for Calvin Klein Cosmetics in Manhattan from 1989 until 2003, then retired to Florida, his childhood home. He died in 2021, exactly fifty years after his "little porno movie," as he described it, began a revolution in gay adult film.

CHAPTER 29

SYLVESTER: QUEEN OF DISCO

During San Francisco's "golden age of gay awakening" in the years from 1975 to 1985, no one better personified the era's raw energy, personal liberation, released sexuality, sheer fun—and ultimate sadness—than Sylvester. By force of overwhelming talent, irrepressible personality and total honesty, he immortalized himself. As the English journalist Stephen Brogan later described him, he was "a star who shined brightly. He only happened once. He was a radical and a visionary in terms of queerness, music and race."

Sylvester was always out, always himself, a visible, proud and unapologetically gay African American who expressed his own sense of self, onstage and off. "I've never been straight," he told one interviewer. For his high school graduation picture in 1969, he wore a blue chiffon prom dress with his coif done up in a beehive hairstyle. Some critics described him as a drag queen, but he disagreed. "I might wear costumes and dress up," he said, "but that's me." Mostly, he was determined to be Sylvester, ignoring any boundaries that would confine him.

Whether his audience was large or small, he never stinted on a performance and was always open and welcoming to fans who came up to him in public. Fame changed him very little, although he acknowledged in 1977, just before his breakthrough success, that he seldom went to bars anymore and had "stopped going to the baths because people want to talk about my songs and I don't go to the baths to *talk*."

Sylvester was born in Los Angeles on September 6, 1947, and his first professional appearance was as a hopeful in a baby contest, which he won. "I got paid for that," he later told an interviewer. His true calling, however, was music, which he embraced all his life. He sang in the gospel choir of his Pentecostal church until he was thirteen years old, quitting, he said, because of the homophobia expressed by members of the congregation. At fifteen, he started going to local gay clubs, making cross-dressing friends who eventually became the Disquotays; the group disbanded in 1970.

Still in Los Angeles, Sylvester met Reggie Dunnigan, who encouraged his move to San Francisco, where he joined the drag hippie performance community of the Cockettes. Their parodies of then-popular culture had already gained a local cult following, which Sylvester only increased; for one of his first performances with the group, he sang the theme song of *The Mickey Mouse Club* wearing a cowgirl skirt. Following a disastrous booking in New York, however, Sylvester left the group to become a solo performer.

It took many years for him to become an overnight sensation. Jann Wenner, founder of *Rolling Stone* magazine, who saw Sylvester with the Cockettes in New York, decided he should be a recording

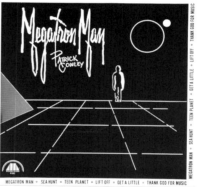

Top: Always out, always himself, a visible, proud and unapologetically gay African American, Sylvester was the indisputable "Queen of Disco." *Photographer unknown. Library of Congress.*

Bottom: Patrick Cowley's hit dance single "Megatron Man" became the first track on the second album his independent company, Megatone Records, released: openly gay music for a gay audience. *Author's collection.*

artist. True to himself, Sylvester showed up at the studio in a "long flowing dress, hair piled high and neckline plunging." A&M Records, home of the *Tijuana Brass*, paid for recording sessions but declined to release the end result. Even Sylvester admitted it "was a mess from the very beginning."

In 1973, Sylvester signed with Blue Thumb Records, but his two albums for them were not successful. Four years later, he recorded *Sylvester*, with back-up vocals by Two Tons O' Fun—future Weather Girls Martha Wash and Izora Rhodes—for Fantasy Records. Presenting him as a rhythm-and-blues singer influenced by dance music, it sold modestly. 1978's *Step II*, however, which showcased his full embrace of the high-energy, sexualized dance music called disco, made him a star of stars.

Step II contained two immediate and enduring music classics: "You Make Me Feel (Mighty Real)" and "Dance (Disco Heat)." Both quickly became no. 1 on Billboard's American dance chart. The album was Sylvester's first with Patrick Cowley, who became his frequent collaborator. Together they perfected San Francisco's Hi-NRG sound, which brought Sylvester success at last. The critic Peter Shapiro later wrote that their work together "pretty much [summed] up the entire disco experience."

Born in Buffalo, New York, in 1950, Cowley moved to San Francisco in 1971. He began experimenting with electronic music equipment, putting together synthetic sounds with those of traditional instruments to create something completely new. He pioneered in other ways, too. For his Megatrone Records label, he created, recorded and released albums of gay music as an openly gay man for an obviously gay audience, including *Menergy* and *Megatron Man*, that celebrated gay sexuality and desire.

Cowley died in 1982, an early victim of the AIDS epidemic, the year that Sylvester released *All I Need* on Megatone Records. It included his immortal Hi-NRG classic "Do Ya Wanna Funk," written by Cowley, and two other singles that reached no. 3 on Billboard's *Disco Action* chart. There was never a secret about who he was: even his music publishing company was named Masculine Music.

Sylvester created two more albums for Megatone and then signed with Warner Brothers Records, which released *Mutual Attraction*, with original cover art by Keith Haring, in 1986. One single from the album, "Someone Like You," became Sylvester's third no. 1 hit; another, "Living for the City," reached no. 2 on Billboard's dance chart. A second album would remain unfinished.

After this joyous success, Sylvester's life became filled with misfortune. Rick Cranmer, his partner, died from AIDS complications in September 1987. Soon after, he noticed symptoms of HIV in himself. As with everything else in his life, he was open and honest about his condition. "Who was I gonna hide the disease from?" he told the *San Francisco Examiner* reporter Barry Walters. "If I kept it a secret, what good would that do? I've been doing

AIDS benefits for many, many years, long before it became fashionable. It would be ridiculous to be secretive about it now."

Despite the adversity, he remained his buoyant self, his sense of humor intact. "I didn't need to take the AIDS antibody test," he said. "I know what I've done. Why would I waste those $90 when I could go shopping?" He became too sick to perform, although he still joined People with AIDS in the 1988 Gay Freedom Parade, using a wheelchair.

The Castro Street Fair, three months later, was "A Tribute to Sylvester"; sadly, he was now too ill to attend. He continued to give interviews, however, to bring attention to the devastation brought by the epidemic, especially to the African American community. Once "an icon of San Francisco nightlife," wrote Walters,

A resident of the neighborhood, Sylvester performed at the Castro Street Fair at no charge, paying the considerable expenses himself. *Photograph by Robert Pruzan. Robert Pruzan Papers (1998-36), GLBT Historical Society.*

he was now "a symbol of a totally different San Francisco—a gay man struggling to stay alive." He died on December 16, 1988, only forty-one years old.

Disco is long gone, but almost everything Sylvester recorded is still vital—and still available—on disc or download, and his brilliance continues to influence performers today as it did in past. His music will live as long as we have ears on our heads and joy in our hearts.

CHAPTER 30

THE MAYOR OF CASTRO STREET

I n 1974, Harvey Milk and Scott Smith gave a block party and invited the immediate world. On August 18, some five thousand people joined them at the first Castro Street Fair to enjoy mimes, clowns and music, chat with friends old and new and visit booths offering food and handicrafts. It was the largest gathering the neighborhood had seen since the California Centennial Celebration held many years before and immediately became one of the major events on the city's LGBTQ+ calendar.

The first fair established many of the fundamentals that have made those that followed great fun. From the beginning, community organizations shared information, vendors sold their goods and local talent entertained the crowds. Fairgoers looked forward to a day spent outside, an occasional glimpse of the odd and unusual and people watching, always the most popular pastime. Attendees shared the results of their hard work at the gym and showed off the latest skin fashions, from newly pierced nipples to tony tattoo art.

Besides hoping a good time would be had by all on a hopefully warm and sunny summer afternoon, Harvey later wrote that he wanted "to promote the area and to show the city the potential power that the gay community has." A street fair with "a great crowd" would display an authentic, vibrant LGBTQ+ neighborhood and demonstrate its economic strength. At the same time, he hoped "to register as many people as we could on that day" to build its political influence.

Born in Woodmere, Long Island, New York, Milk attended teachers' college, served four years in the navy, taught high school and worked as a

statistician for an insurance company and as a researcher for an investment firm before he and Scott moved to San Francisco in 1972. The next year, they opened a camera store at 575 Castro Street, which quickly developed into the neighborhood's "city hall," the place where people always seemed to gather to discuss the latest gossip, news, problems and concerns.

The neighborhood was not as welcoming as it might have been. Frustrated and angered by the opposition that newly opened gay-owned shops were receiving from the long-established Eureka Valley Merchants Association, Milk and a few other gay businessmen founded the Castro Village Association (CVA) in 1973. Later that year, he ran for the San Francisco Board of Supervisors as an openly gay man. Harvey lost that first election, but he had found his next career as an advocate and political leader.

Milk never denied the power of protests, boycotts, picket lines and marches, but he realized not everyone could join one to effect change. "If you believe in the gay movement," he wrote, "then you must do more than just talk about it. You must make sure that all your friends are also registered and that they do vote. Without that, as the bottom line, gay rights will forever be something sought after." Only some three hundred people registered to vote at the first fair, but it was a start.

Harvey believed that voting was something people could do easily; they did not even need to leave their homes to make their choices and return

Opposite: Nothing was—and is—more fun at the Castro Street Fair than people watching. *Photograph by Crawford Barton. Crawford Barton Papers (1993-11), GLBT Historical Society.*

Above: The first time he ran for office in 1973, Harvey Milk, who campaigned as a long-haired, gay hippie, placed tenth in a field of thirty-two candidates. *Photograph by Crawford Barton. Crawford Barton Papers (1993-11), GLBT Historical Society.*

their ballots. He and everyone who worked at Castro Camera became registrars, and he made sure of an ample supply of voter registration forms for visitors to the store. Its front windows turned into a community bulletin board, covered with announcements of upcoming civil rights demonstrations, protests, meetings and events. Milk soon became known as the "Mayor of Castro Street."

Speaking out, organizing and registering voters seemed to work. In 1975, Harvey finished seventh in citywide elections for supervisor, getting the highest number of votes of anybody running who was not an incumbent. The next year, when he ran for the state assembly, he was only narrowly defeated. In 1977—his third candidacy in three years—with contenders now running in neighborhoods and not citywide, he became the first openly gay man elected to public office in California.

The *New York Times* recognized the great importance of Harvey's election. In its November 6, 1977 issue, it stated, "What San Francisco is today, and

Milk's headquarters for all of his campaigns was his camera store on Castro Street, where people could register to vote. *Photograph by Henri Leleu. Henry Leleu Papers (1997-13), GLBT Historical Society.*

what it is becoming, reflects both the energy and organization of the gay community and its developing effort toward integration in the political processes of the American city best known for innovation in life styles." In an inspiring ceremony the following January, Harvey was sworn in with the first single mother, the first Chinese American and the first African American woman ever elected to the board of supervisors.

Throughout his political career, Milk spoke of the need for hope and community. The importance of the first he explained with great clarity at a meeting of the California Democratic Council on March 10, 1978, two months after he took office and eight months before he was assassinated. For too many young gay people, he said,

> *The only thing they have to look forward to is hope. And you have to give them hope. Hope for a better world, hope for a better tomorrow, hope for a better place to come to if the pressures at home are too great. Hope that all will be all right. Without hope, not only gays, but the blacks, the seniors, the handicapped, the us'es, the us'es will give up. And if you help elect to the central committee and other offices, more gay people, that gives a green light to all who feel disenfranchised, a green light to move forward. It means hope to a nation that has given up, because if a gay person makes it, the doors are open to everyone.*

Later that year, in a campaign brochure he distributed at the Castro Street Fair, he explained his feelings about community and how the event helped to create it:

> *Everyone needs a sense of belonging and neighborliness and the chance to celebrate the joys of living where we live....Every neighborhood should have a street fair, and everyone should have a chance to work with her/his neighbors to make one happen close to home.*

The world has changed since the first Castro Street Fair and Harvey's time in public office. Then, cell phones were found in jails, not pockets, and laptops were for dances, not homework. Physical intimacy between consenting adults was illegal, and people who enjoyed it could be fired from their jobs for no other reason than that. No longer. Harvey succeeded in showing the city and the world the political, social and economic importance of the Castro and the LGBTQ+ communities. His ideas and his example have been followed by communities everywhere to bring reform and progress.

The changes Harvey helped effect are now dramatically on display at the fair, which Mark Barabak described in the *San Francisco Chronicle* as an event where drag queens mingle "with uniformed police officers and local politicians hoping to win points with an important San Francisco constituency." More than anything else, it continues to prove the understanding in Harvey's words of wisdom to "let people see the truth about who gays are, and in so doing give gay and other disenfranchised people hope." There is nothing like an afternoon spent with one hundred thousand intimate friends.

CHAPTER 31

RANDY SHILTS: REPORTING GAY HISTORY

Before AIDS had its name, before it had the attention of the media, the government or even the gay community, Randy Shilts (1951–1994) was bringing information about it to the notice of the public. Reporting for the *San Francisco Chronicle*, where he was the first openly gay reporter to be hired by a major American newspaper—and the first to cover the gay community full time—he eventually persuaded his bosses to let him focus exclusively on the malady.

One of the few journalists to recognize the growing epidemic as an important national issue, Shilts discovered there were in fact two important stories not being reported: the tragedy of human suffering and the lives being destroyed in their prime and the unmovable indifference of government, medicine, health care and social systems to a major—and growing—public health crisis.

"With a passion I have rarely seen equaled in the business, Randy pushed, wheedled and cajoled until his AIDS stories made their way from the back pages of the *Chronicle* to the front page," said Susan Sward not long after his death. "He hurled himself into the stories he wrote." Shilts himself was more modest about his accomplishments. "Any good reporter could have done this story," he said later, "but I think the reason I did it, and no one else did, is because I am gay. It was happening to people I cared about and loved."

The work Shilts was doing to report the AIDS epidemic led him to write *And the Band Played On.* Published in 1987, when a diagnosis of AIDS still meant certain death, the book was the first serious attempt to chronicle the disease in the United States. More importantly, however, Shilts detailed why and how so many institutions and organizations, both public and private, designed "to promote the general Welfare, and secure the Blessings of Liberty to ourselves and our Posterity," failed to confront it.

His findings were both shocking and unsurprising. By doing so little for so long, public officials, business leaders, medical experts, researchers and others in positions of authority enabled the disease to spread unrestrained during the first five years after its appearance, the result of their loathing of the gay community, their focus on ideological preaching instead of public health, petty squabbles, turf wars, scientific jealousies and rivalries, self-serving interests and failures of political vision, principle and equity.

Shilts spent his entire career in investigative journalism, almost always writing about gay issues. After earning his degree in journalism from the University of Oregon, he went to work as the northwest correspondent for the *Advocate* and then moved to the Bay Area to cover city politics and gay issues for local radio and television stations. He joined the staff of the *Chronicle* just before his first book, *The Mayor of Castro Street*, was published in 1982.

Mayor not only shared the life and career of Harvey Milk, the first openly gay man to be elected to public office in the United States, but it also told the story of LBGTQ+ society and politics in the 1970s. Many praised the book as "the definitive story of the man whose personal life, public career, and tragic assassination mirrored the dramatic and unprecedented emergence of the gay community in America."

Shilts, however, considered it to be "an investigative piece on the mechanics of big city government in all its expedient, back-biting splendor," one that "employs standard, professional reportorial techniques in the gathering and verifying of all the information cited." First published almost thirty-five years ago, it has never been out of print.

Conduct Unbecoming, the book Shilts wrote after *And the Band Played On*, carried on his examination of institutional and social attitudes toward members of the LGBTQ+ communities. Published in 1993, the year before he died, it chronicled the experiences of lesbians and gays in the United States military from the end of the Korean War to onset of Desert Storm.

In the book, based on extensive research that included more than one thousand interviews, Shilts documented not only how institutionalized homophobia led to the mistreatment of gay men and lesbians in the armed services but also the hypocrisy of an organization that only selectively

Randy Shilts (*right*) became "the first openly gay reporter with a gay 'beat' in the American mainstream press." *Photograph by Robert Pruzan. Robert Pruzan Papers (1998-36), GLBT Historical Society.*

enforced its ban on homosexuals in uniform. It remains a classic example of investigative journalism.

Our world is different than the one Shilts investigated—and dissected—in his three books. Unlike politicians and other professionals at the time Milk ran his election campaigns, members of the LGBTQ+ communities now can be open about themselves as public office seekers—or as film stars, newscasters, corporate officers, even professional athletes. AIDS is no longer ignored by public and private institutions. Lesbians, gays, bisexuals and transgender Americans can serve openly in the military.

All of this may seem to make Shilts's work dated and irrelevant to the present, but he did more than write the biography of any individual or present the story of any single public policy. He revealed how bigotry, hypocrisy and sheer indifference to others become institutionalized, how they deeply damage human lives and how they increase human suffering. Because only the names of the governments, the organizations and the communities left to fend for themselves ever seem to change, Shilts's findings are as vital today as when he first shared them.

CHAPTER 32

BOBBI CAMPBELL: AIDS POSTER BOY

B obbi Campbell (1952–1984) was only thirty in 1982, when he and playwright Dan Turner (1948–1990) brought together a group of people to found what became the People With AIDS (PWAs) Self-Empowerment Movement. The term *AIDS* did not yet exist, so during the first few months, he spoke and wrote about having Kaposi's Sarcoma (KS), the disease that first brought attention to what was still an undiscovered epidemic with global implications.

The group had what then seemed like revolutionary ideas. First it rejected the commonly used term *KS victim*. As Campbell explained, "'KS victim' means the bus has run over you and you're lying there in the street, flattened....I do not feel like a victim." Then it argued for self-empowerment, for people with the disease to participate actively in the response to the crisis they were caught up in. It was the first organization created by and for people with what in a few months became known as AIDS.

The previous October, Campbell became only the sixteenth young man in San Francisco to be diagnosed with Kaposi's Sarcoma, until then a rare skin cancer seen mostly in elderly people with compromised immune systems. Because of his professional and personal interest in gay men's sexual health, he realized that the entire community needed to become aware of what was being labeled, with shame and censure when it was mentioned at all, as "gay cancer."

How to do that, when many people and most media were denying a serious reality or ignoring it completely? Campbell created and posted San

Before it was named or even identified, Bobbi Campbell was the first person to announce publicly that he was a person with what would become known as AIDS. *Photograph by Marie Ueda. Marie Ueda Collection (2006-12), GLBT Historical Society.*

Francisco's first AIDS awareness poster. The same month that he received his diagnosis, he put a notice of the illness, including pictures of his KS lesions, in the window of the Star Pharmacy at Eighteenth and Castro Streets, the intergalactic crossroads of the gay world. He urged those with similar lesions to get medical attention.

Less than six weeks later, Campbell wrote an article that appeared on page one of the December 10, 1981 issue of the *Sentinel*, a biweekly community newspaper. In the piece, headlined "Nurse's Own 'Gay Cancer' Story" and titled "I WILL SURVIVE," he began with a simple, extraordinary statement that, because of the stigma many already associated with the disease and some with homosexuality itself, almost no one at the time was willing to make: "I'm Bobbi Campbell, and I have 'gay cancer.'"

"Let me tell you something about myself," he continued. "I'm a 29-year-old, white, gay man who's lived in the City for six years. I work as a Registered Nurse at Ralph K. Davies Medical Center, and I'm studying at the University of California at San Francisco (UCSF) for a Master's Degree in Nursing as an Adult Health Nurse Practitioner. When UCSF's Graduate Division asked me what my focus of study would be, I wrote that I was most interested in specializing in gay health care."

The most important contribution he could make to his chosen field now, he believed, was to tell others about the very real risks they were facing. "I've become so active in publicizing KS and the other gay illnesses to friends and media that I've taken to referring to myself sardonically as the 'Kaposi's Sarcoma Poster Boy.' He concluded his article, which became the first a series, with an urgent, personal appeal. "I'm writing because I have a determination to live. You do, too—don't you?"

Campbell more than deserved his title as the "Kaposi's Sarcoma Poster Boy." The next year, after joining the Sisters of Perpetual Indulgence as Sister Florence Nightmare, RN, he and Sister Roz Erection (aka Baruch Golden), also a registered nurse, led the group that created *Play Fair!* While the brochure may not have contained the first guidelines for safer sex written for gay men by gay men, it almost certainly was the first to share information about STDs with humor, even drollness, as it presented extremely serious and practical advice.

Using frank, simple language and easy-to-understand, sex-positive terminology, the brochure described the STDs being found in San Francisco's gay communities, explained "How You Get It," shared symptoms to look for and included a "list of gay-sensitive places to get diagnosed and/or treated." It also clarified that "mysterious forms of cancer and pneumonia are now lurking among us, too." HIV/AIDS had not been identified yet, so it described KS, "the so-called 'gay cancer,'" and "Pneumocystis pneumonia—'gay pneumonia.'"

Play Fair! was so well received that it was reprinted within just a few months of its first appearance. It quickly became a landmark document in not only the fight against HIV/AIDS but also the efforts to educate gay people about the many risks to their health and well-being, including guilt, the one STD that was "subject to home remedies." Symptoms, it advised, appear "from 2 to 3 years of age and persist in many cases throughout life." The cure: "Respect and love yourself and others."

Campbell now devoted more and more of his time to gay men's health issues. In early 1982, he and Turner also attended what became the founding

As Sister Florence Nightmare, Campbell coauthored *Play Fair!* (1982), one of the earliest safer sex guides written by and for gay men. *Photograph by Robert Pruzan. Robert Pruzan Papers (1998-36), GLBT Historical Society.*

meeting of the KS/AIDS Foundation, later renamed the San Francisco AIDS Foundation; Campbell then served on the board. He also became involved with the Shanti Project, which provided emotional support to people diagnosed with AIDS. Awareness, he soon realized, was not enough, and he began to argue that people with AIDS had to speak up and out for themselves.

The next year, Campbell, now known as the "AIDS Poster Boy," helped organize the first AIDS Candlelight March, held simultaneously in San Francisco and New York. On May 2, 1983, he and some ten thousand people marched from the Castro to Civic Center behind a banner reading, "Fighting for Our Lives," proclaiming to the world that gay men, even when confronted with ignorance, disdain and indifference, "do not go gentle into that good night." Less than a month later, the statement's four powerful words expanded into a statement of principles and actions.

During the last week of May, Campbell and Turner attended the Fifth Annual Lesbian and Gay Health Conference in Denver. There, they met with some dozen other PWAs who, together, created a statement of truths, now known as the Denver Principles, that summarized the rights and responsibilities of health care providers, PWAs and anyone who was concerned or touched by the epidemic.

Presented during the closing session of the conference, the Denver Principles rejected any attempts to label PWAs "as 'victims,' a term which implies defeat." In addition to demanding vital reforms in the practice of medicine itself, it insisted that medical professionals see PWAs as individuals, as "whole people," not as cases or "'patients,' a term which implies passivity, helplessness, and dependence upon the care of others."

As "People With AIDS," they demanded the right "to live as full and satisfying sexual and emotional lives as anyone else" and to receive "quality medical treatment and quality social service provision without discrimination of any form." They also demanded to obtain "full explanations of all medical procedures and risks" and "to make informed decisions about their lives," among other important reforms. Above all, they asserted their right "to human respect" and "to die—and to LIVE—in dignity."

The importance of the Denver Principles cannot be stressed enough. Never before had a group of individuals with the same disease come together to assert their right to participate in the decisions that would determine the rest of their lives. Its basic tenets have influenced how all of us are involved in our own health care and transformed the way that care, as well as the social services and legal protections needed to support it, is provided and received, benefiting millions of individuals during difficult times.

Verifying his status as the "AIDS Poster Boy," Campbell and his "friend" Bobby Hilliard—the magazine apparently was unable to embrace them as lovers—appeared on the August 8, 1983 cover of *Newsweek*. The article, "Gay America: Sex, Politics and the Impact of AIDS," its second cover story about the epidemic, showed no more understanding of the health crisis than any other mainstream publication, but it still did better than a president who did not mention AIDS publicly until two years later.

Campbell worked tirelessly for change until he died. On July 15, 1984, he spoke at the National March for Lesbian and Gay Rights, held during the Democratic National Convention in San Francisco. He was introduced as "a feminist, a registered Democrat and a Person with AIDS." Telling his audience that he had hugged his boyfriend on the cover of *Newsweek*, he then kissed Hilliard onstage, "to show Middle America that gay love is beautiful."

Exactly a month after his speech, after three and a half years living with HIV/AIDS, he was gone. Two days later, Castro Street was closed for people to gather there to mourn his passing, celebrate his life and honor his great contributions to human dignity. In 2014, a Castro Street History Walk plaque commemorated him and the day he posted the "first notice about 'gay cancer' on Star Pharmacy's window at 498 Castro Street." In 2022, he was selected as an honoree for San Francisco's Rainbow Honor Walk.

CHAPTER 33

TOM WADDELL: GAY OLYMPIAN

No one ever brought more of the true Olympian spirit to San Francisco than Tom Waddell (1937–1987). As the Olympic Charter holds, he built "a peaceful and better world by educating youth through sport practiced without discrimination of any kind," and he also strove to "promote mutual understanding with a spirit of friendship, solidarity and fair play."

Waddell's vision, in fact, was even more powerful. He had a goal of furthering, as he explained it, "sport based on inclusion rather than exclusion" and sport based on equality and universal participation. His Gay Olympic Games would bring people together to know each other and challenge each other to excel.

The games were held for the first time in San Francisco in 1982. Not only did they celebrate people, but they also enabled them to be honest and open with each other about their sexuality. Anybody could participate, with no regard to race, gender, age, national origin or sexual orientation—and with no minimum qualifying standards or even athletic ability. The only criteria was the desire to compete and to be one's best.

For Waddell's efforts, the United States Olympic Committee took him to court twice. The word *olympic* has been part of the English language since at least the late sixteenth century, but it became the exclusive property of the United States Olympic Committee in 1978, a gift of the United States Congress. Nineteen days before the opening ceremonies, USOC received the court injunction it sought to forbid Waddell from using the term.

Even though it allowed—and allows—pancake, math, frog, pattern, librarian, urology and doggie olympics, among others, without apparent damage or injury to its reputation or world standing, the committee forced Waddell to delete *olympic* from his organization's name and everything associated with it, including posters, banners, programs, flags, souvenirs and award medals.

The case was argued all the way to the Supreme Court of the United States, which ruled in a 5–4 decision in 1987 that USOC had "the legal authority to bar a homosexual rights group from using the generic word 'olympic' in the name of its games." By then, USOC had also sued Waddell for its court costs of some $96,000 and placed a lien on his home.

Physician and decathlete Tom Waddell created an international community of athletes as founder of the Gay Games, first staged in 1982. *Photograph by Robert Pruzan. Robert Pruzan Papers (1998-36), GLBT Historical Society.*

Despite the obstacles created by the Olympic Committee to thwart them, the first Gay Games were a tremendous success. Many considered the opening ceremony at Kezar Stadium in San Francisco's Golden Gate Park to be "one of the most uplifting events in LGBT history." It marked the beginning of a week of participation by 1,350 athletes from twelve countries in seventeen sports. Lives were changed, and "it was clear the Gay Games would be held again."

A true Olympian, Waddell excelled in many fields. He was born Thomas Flubacher on November 1, 1937, in Paterson, New Jersey. After his parents separated, he went to live with Gene and Hazel Waddell, who later adopted him and encouraged an interest in sports. At Springfield College in Massachusetts, he joined both the gymnastics and football teams. He was a physical education major, too, until the unexpected death of his college roommate and best friend, which moved him to switch to premed.

Waddell graduated from the New Jersey College of Medicine in 1965. The next year, he was drafted into the army. Two years later, when he received orders to ship out to Vietnam, he told his commanding officer that he was morally opposed to the war and preferred to go to prison. Instead of court-martialing him, however, the military sent him to train, with other service members, for the summer Olympic Games in Mexico City.

The parade of athletes at the first Gay Games exemplified the diversity, sportsmanship and inclusiveness that the Olympics supposedly aspired to achieve. *Photograph by Robert Pruzan. Robert Pruzan Papers (1998-36), GLBT Historical Society.*

He placed sixth among thirty-three competitors in the decathlon, an outstanding achievement even for an athlete with years of rigorous preparation. Waddell, who had not been in a decathlon for more than five years, had prepared for a negligible three months.

An individual of wide-ranging interests and concerns, Waddell embraced the cause of human rights his entire life. In 1965, he traveled to Selma, Alabama, to participate in the civil rights demonstrations there. While still in the army, he openly criticized the Vietnam War. At the 1968 Olympics, he supported the actions of two American athletes who were harshly criticized for giving the Black Power salute during their award ceremony.

Even before same-sex intimacy became legal in California, he was openly gay. In 1976, he and Charles Deaton became the first gay partners profiled in *People* magazine's "Couples" section. As a healer of human suffering, a defender of sportsmanship and a champion for human dignity and equal rights, his is a place of distinction on San Francisco's Rainbow Honor Walk.

Waddell died on July 11, 1987, but the Gay Games continue as a living tribute to this remarkable man and role model. In 1990, more than seven thousand athletes participated in Gay Games III, held in Vancouver. Four years later, New York's Gay Games IV, with almost eleven thousand athletes from six continents, became the largest amateur sporting event in history. Participants and spectators alike continue to be inspired by Waddell's vision of inclusion and participation.

CHAPTER 34

GILBERT BAKER:
FOREVER LET US HOLD OUR BANNER HIGH

G reen carnations. Red neckties. Violet corsages. These colors and symbols were used for many years by gay men and lesbians, often strangers in the night, to identify each other across a crowded room or in a public place. Until Gilbert Baker (1951–2017) created the Rainbow Flag in 1978, however, there was no single emblem or icon to join LGBTQ+ people as members of a world community, wherever they might be, much less one that validated and honored them everywhere.

Baker grew up in Parsons, Kansas, not far from the famous barnyard, which was actually in Culver City, where Dorothy Gale supposedly sang "Over the Rainbow" for the first time. Because he was drawn to art and fashion as a child, not to cows and corn like his peers, he did not exactly fit into their bucolic world.

The chance to follow his own yellow brick road came in 1970, when he was drafted into the army. Stationed in San Francisco, where he served as a medic, he found the welcoming community he sought. After his honorable discharge in 1972, Baker stayed in the city. He became involved with the social and political causes of the time, using his artistry to create banners for anti-war protests and pro-gay marches.

No one combined sequined couture and street theater to greater effect than Gilbert, so in 1978, when he was asked to create a visual affirmation of San Francisco's LGBTQ+ communities, he was ready. His simple and elegant solution: a banner with eight equal stripes to show our unity, our diversity and the sources of our strength. "We needed something to express our joy, our beauty, our power," he explained later, "and the rainbow did that."

Although others helped him dye the material, Baker sewed the original flag himself. Each of the eight stripes represented a different quality. From top to bottom, they were pink (sexuality), red (life), orange (healing), yellow (sunlight), green (nature), turquoise (magic), indigo/blue (serenity) and violet (spirit).

Gilbert displayed his newly created banner publicly from the flagpoles in United Nations Plaza for the first time on June 25, 1978, for the San Francisco Gay Freedom Day Parade. "When it went up and the wind finally took it out of my hands, it blew my mind," he remembered later. "I saw immediately how everyone around me owned the flag. I thought, 'It's better than I ever dreamed.'"

After Harvey Milk's assassination in November 1978, the parade committee voted to adopt the new rainbow flag as a symbol of the community's unity and strength, not only in joy but also in

Gilbert Baker, also known as Sister Chanel 2001 and Busty Ross, created the unifying symbol of the modern LGBTQ+ movement for San Francisco's 1978 Pride Parade. *Photograph by Gareth Watkins. Wikimedia.*

adversity. The pink stripe was dropped when, according to Baker, his flag manufacturer "ran out of pink dye." The violet band was removed so that the flag could be displayed evenly along the parade route, three colors on each side of the street. In 1989, the International Congress of Flag Makers recognized the Rainbow Flag.

Today, many variations of the flag exist. Some people add a black stripe to honor those lost to AIDS. There also are versions with different colored stripes or symbols added to represent bisexual people, transgender people, pansexuals, asexuals, bears, lesbians, genderfluid pride, leather pride, trigenders and other communities within our community. All follow Baker's original design, but only his universally unites us all.

CHAPTER 35

GEORGE CHOY: PASSIONATE ACTIVIST

George Choy was a passionate advocate of civil and human rights for members of the LGBTQ+ communities of San Francisco and around the world. Driven by the belief that we are "part of the family, too," he became, as one friend eulogized him, "a constant supportive presence who delivered with action, an activist impatient with injustice, but who nevertheless possessed the rare gift of forgiving."

Born on February 6, 1960, Choy liked to say that he was an Acqueerian. He came out to himself during the summer after he graduated from San Francisco's Mission High School, just before leaving to attend San Jose State University. Instead of feeling guilty, "instead of lying to myself and others," he told himself to "be happy and love who[m] you want."

His self-awareness, insight and perception were transformative. "I was free," he wrote later. "I no longer hid from my straight schoolmates about my sexuality." He told his two closest friends, hoping they would "support me." Both did. He was best man at their weddings, and they remained lifelong confidants.

Choy saw the need for activism early on. He grew up in Chinatown, across the street from the International Hotel. The Filipino seniors who lived in the hotel, which was once the heart of San Francisco's Philippine community, were forcibly evicted for an "urban renewal" project during the 1970s. Their protests to save their homes and preserve their community—which at one time included ten blocks of low-cost housing, stores, restaurants, markets and other businesses that supported a neighborhood of some ten thousand people—left an indelible impression on him.

Believing that we all belong to a larger world than our ethnic, religious or social identifications create for us, Choy wanted to make connections across artificial barriers to show our common humanity. This goal propelled his activism. Especially committed to achieving full civil and human rights for LGBTQ+ Asians, he became an early and active member of San Francisco's Gay Asian Pacific Alliance (GAPA).

Choy also was vocal in support of queer youth, an often-neglected minority within a minority. In the spring of 1990, he was asked to lead GAPA's effort to pass Project 10, a measure to provide much-needed counseling services for San Francisco's LGBTQ+ public school students. Although he believed that "living in San Francisco helped a lot of straight people deal with gays," he also knew that there were still "those who experienced gay-related violence," including some "attacked by family members because of their sexuality."

The proposal faced numerous hurdles, with opponents claiming that it was unnecessary, inappropriate and not fundable. Choy, however, immediately recognized its importance for all students, especially for gay Asians. "We have to be there," he said, "to make sure they know that there are Gay Asians." "They" included not only members of the school board and the mostly white gay activists who supported the proposal but also Asian Christian fundamentalists, who had come out in full force against it, arguing simply that the service was not needed because there were "no gay Asians."

During the critical meeting at which the board was to vote on the proposal, Choy made an impassioned plea for it to pass. He argued that gay Asians were "not to be taken for granted" but to be "loved, saved, and protected." In May 1990, the board of education decided unanimously to implement Project 10 the following September. "This program," said Kevin Gogin, the first counselor hired, "will send a message that all people are important, no matter who they are."

Choy's efforts to realize human rights for gay Asians went far beyond San Francisco. In 1991, GAPA supported a lawsuit against a public youth activity center in Tokyo that denied the use of its facilities to OCCUR, a local LGBTQ+ organization. When members of OCCUR visited the Bay Area to gain support for their anti-discrimination case against the Tokyo government, he organized press conferences, held meetings and got local political figures involved. He then traveled to Japan to speak about human rights for gays to large audiences in Tokyo and Osaka, one of San Francisco's sister cities.

At the same time, Choy worked as GAPA's community HIV project liaison. He next became the outreach coordinator for the organization's Community Health Project, which provided direct support services to gay Asians and

**George Choy
(1960-1993)**

Passionate activist for queer
Asians and Pacific Islanders and
AIDS awareness who was
instrumental in bringing LGBT
counseling programs into San
Francisco public high schools

rainbow honor walk

George Choy

George Choy's plaque on the Rainbow Honor Walk recognizes his passionate activism for queer Asians and Pacific Islanders and his successful work to increase AIDS awareness, among his other accomplishments. *Rainbow Honor Walk.*

Pacific Islanders that included prevention, education, early intervention, HIV case management, emotional and practical support and direct care. He also was an active and ardent member of ACT UP. More than anything else, he showed what a single individual can do for the benefit of us all.

Not long before he died of AIDS on September 10, 1993, Choy spoke of what he had learned since that summer after high school. "Deep inside each of us," he told his audience, "burns a special flame…which other people misunderstand.…But we, as gay and lesbian people, understand…that we have a special capacity to love one another. We understand that this love is real and valid. We understand that this special flame will light the way for us.…Continue to fan the flame, strong, proud, and just."

CHAPTER 36

TREVOR HAILEY: IN THE FOOTSTEPS OF HISTORY

No one knows when or where their aha moment will come to them. For some of us, our great inspiration is a chance remark, an unexpected encounter or a fortuitous occurrence. For Castro resident Trevor Hailey, creator of "Cruisin' the Castro," the first LGBTQ+ experience of its kind in San Francisco, it was a lecture she attended given by Shirley Fong-Torres, the longtime leader of Chinatown walking tours, at San Francisco State University.

At the time, Haley was taking graduate courses in recreation and leisure, so Fong-Torres's remarks and her example particularly resonated with her. "It was like a lightbulb went off," Hailey said later. She began researching the history of LGBTQ+ San Francisco, especially the Castro. "That's when I discovered we even had a history," she remembered during an interview. "Until then, I thought we'd all sprung full-bloom from rocks."

What was the city's LGBTQ+ past? How did the Castro, its most famous and influential LGBTQ+ neighborhood, come to be? Who were its most important residents? What happened here and where? "I knew right then," she later said, "that's what I wanted to do"—share what she had learned.

Born Dorothy Evelyn Fondren in 1941, Hailey grew up in Jackson, Mississippi. Although she knew from an early age that she was not exactly like all the other children, she was not sure what to do about it or how. Like many before her—and after—she joined the navy to see the world and to find herself. Stationed first in New York, she then transferred to the Naval Hospital Oakland in 1972, where she served as a nurse.

After discovering San Francisco, she later stated, she "didn't look back." When she completed her service, she began a new career as a real estate

During her years as a tour guide, Trevor Hailey explained "how and why San Francisco got to be literally the Gay Mecca of the world" to some thirty thousand people. *Photograph by Ron Williams. Courtesy of Ron Williams.*

agent, working for the next ten years at a brokerage just a few doors from Milk's camera store on Castro Street. There she watched the neighborhood come into its own, experiencing the triumph of Harvey Milk's election, the tragedy of his murder, the devastation of the AIDS epidemic, the resilience of the community and so much more.

Hailey's first walking tour was in 1989. From the beginning, she explained not only the historic significance of a place but also the importance of what happened there. The buildings she pointed out along the way might have been interesting in themselves, but of greater moment, they were where people lived and worked, played and partied, where they came together to protest discrimination and to secure the human rights previously denied to members of our LGBTQ+ communities.

When she passed 575 Castro Street, for example, she did not simply point out that this was where Harvey Milk once had his camera shop, but she explained how he became the first openly gay candidate elected to the board of supervisors, where he advanced human rights for LGBTQ+ San Franciscans. Pink Triangle Park was not only the home of a memorial to lesbians and gays lost to the Holocaust but also a sentinel to proclaim that such horror must never happen again.

After sixteen years, Hailey retired in 2005. By then, she had led some four thousand groups of locals and tourists through the Castro's and San Francisco's history, sometimes having done her four-hour tours seven days a week.

Was it worth it? She thought it was. "Gay people leave with their self-image improved. And those from the alternative lifestyle, or what I call my straight clients, leave far better educated; bless their hearts they have not been given the respect of getting the right information about our community." Besides, she said, "If we don't write our own history, someone else will and we won't like what they had to say."

When Hailey died in 2007, the community mourned its great loss. "Trevor was an institution in our community," said *San Francisco Bay Times* publisher Betty Sullivan, a friend of Hailey's who organized her memorial service. Her "goals were to educate and convey the history of and accurate information about the LGBT community, to locals as well as those from afar." No one can say she did not succeed, leaving a history and a heritage woven deeply into the hearts of all who followed her.

CHAPTER 37

KEN JONES: EQUALITY AND INCLUSION FOR ALL

W hen Ken Jones moved to the Castro fifty years ago, the world, the city and the neighborhood were very different places. Known even then as a gayborhood that attracted thousands with promises of openness, acceptance and sexual freedom, the Castro also had a reputation for not being welcoming to many women or people of color. Jones remembered that as a Black man, he felt comfortable living there, but over time, he realized that progress required LGBTQ+ activism to "look just like our community." He became, in his own words, "kind of the father of diversity."

Born in Paterson, New Jersey, on November 9, 1950, Jones left for San Diego in 1969 to enter the navy. After surviving three tours of duty in Vietnam and being decorated for his service, he concluded his time in the armed forces at the naval base on Treasure Island. Honorably discharged in 1972 as a yeoman first class/YN1 (E-6), he moved across the Bay to San Francisco, where he rented an apartment at Noe and Eighteenth Streets in the heart of the Castro.

That same year, Jones joined the staff at UCSF as manager of grant expenditures and reports. In 1978, he met Konstantin Berlandt (1946–1994), who was working there as a data entry clerk. Unlike the homophiles of the 1950s and '60s, who sought mainstream understanding and assimilation for the gay communities, Berlandt was a gay liberationist who advocated for direct political action and for change through visibility, protest and confrontation, if necessary, an "out of the bars and in your face" activism.

Berlandt came to liberation early on. In 1965, still a student, he wrote the first article about the gay community ever published in the *Daily Californian*, "2,700 Homosexuals at Cal." During the American Psychiatric Association's annual meeting in 1970, held in San Francisco less than a year after the Stonewall Riots, he wore a bright red dress when he and other demonstrators interrupted the proceedings to protest the organization's diagnosis of homosexuality as a "sexual deviation" and a "mental disorder."

Now involved with the Gay Freedom Day Parade, Berlandt asked Jones for his opinion of a flyer for an upcoming committee meeting. "When I pointed out to him the lack of diversity in the all-white all-male images," Jones later told the journalist Hank Trout, "he insisted I attend that meeting to discuss my concerns." By the time the meeting ended, he was responsible for "getting more under-represented or non-represented segments of the community to march with the People of Color Contingent and to join in the parade planning process."

The year 1978, when Jones began volunteering with the parade, was pivotal not only for the organization but also for LGBTQ+ San Francisco. For the first time, Gilbert Baker's rainbow flag appeared at the entrance to the city's civic center. For the first time, the San Francisco Gay Freedom Day Marching Band and Twirling Corps inspired spectators. For the only time, Harvey Milk rode in the parade as the first openly gay man elected to public office in California; his assassination the following November devastated but also galvanized LGBTQ+ communities everywhere.

Among the difficult tasks facing the organization was determining how to represent different LGBTQ+ communities in its name as well as its membership. Finally deciding to include both the terms *gay* and *lesbian* in the name of the parade—*gay* once applied to both women and men—it took months of conversation to agree on the order they would take; the discussion about adding the term *bisexual* was also prolonged.

Jones became president of SF Pride in 1985, the organization's first Black leader and one of the few people of color to lead any Pride organization. His hard work to make the group look more like the community by bringing "a majority of new, non-traditional members into the planning process" was showing success, but the challenges facing the group during his time in office, across some of the darkest days of the AIDS epidemic, were especially daunting.

At the same time, Jones volunteered at the Kaposi's Sarcoma Research and Education Foundation, created in 1982. After it became the San Francisco AIDS Foundation two years later, Jones served as director of volunteer

Across his long career as an activist, Ken Jones worked to bring diversity to LGBTQ+ organizations, including Pride, where he served as its first African American chair. *https://www.kenjonessf.com.*

services and management. To enable the group to reflect the community's diverse people and viewpoints, the same goal he had at Pride, he helped form the Third World AIDS Advisory Committee. In 1985, the year he became Pride's president, he also organized the group's first 100-Mile Bike-a-Thon for AIDS.

Jones also became the Northern California cochair of the California LIFE AIDS Lobby, established in 1986, and was "actively engaged in writing pro-LGBT legislation, lobbying, and killing bad legislation." At the same time, Jones became one of the key organizers in the boycotts against the Castro bars that enforced discriminatory admission policies against women and people of color. The need to include all LGBTQ+ people in the community's public affairs and places remained a goal across all his activism.

In 1989, Jones was diagnosed with HIV. Two years later, saddened and outraged by the police beating of Rodney King in Southern California, he left Pride to work for police reform. As his health began to decline, he participated less and less as an activist, but in the early 2000s, he was again able to forcefully champion inclusion and equality. In 2009, after a BART police officer killed Oscar Grant, he was appointed a member of the citizen review board for the BART Police Department.

To the end of his life on January 13, 2021, Jones gave of himself in whatever ways he could. An ordained deacon at San Francisco's City of Refuge United Church of Christ, he officiated at weddings all over the world and shared his unique knowledge, personal experiences and insights about the city's LGBTQ+ communities on guided tours of the Castro. His contributions to their progress toward visibility, equality, inclusion and participation will endure, woven deeply into the fabric of place and people that is LGBTQ+ San Francisco.

CHAPTER 38

FELICIA ELIZONDO: VIETNAM VETERAN, TRANSGENDER RIGHTS ACTIVIST

F or many people, putting together the pieces of the puzzle of who they are can be relatively easy. Self-awareness, support from family and friends, easily available information and experimentation help us to become us. Not so for Felicia Elizondo. Despite all the prejudice, inaccuracy and obstacles put in her way, however, she came to not only realize her true self but also find the strength and the courage to live an authentic life.

Growing up, Elizondo struggled to understand who she was. Born in San Angelo, Texas, on July 23, 1946, she was identified on her birth certificate as male and baptized as Felipe. At an early age, she knew she was different from the children around her, but she did not yet understand what exactly that meant for her. They called her a "sissy," and she believed them. "There's no other way that I could feel just what I was feeling."

Being a "sissy" then had only one explanation. "I thought I was gay, but I wasn't." Information about sexuality, especially for young people, was difficult to find and often untenable in the homophobic 1950s, so she learned that "being gay was against the law, and it was sick, and mental." She never considered that she might be transgender "because I didn't know the meaning of transgender or transsexual at the time," she told Anita Whites of the Veterans History Project in 2007. Hardly anyone did.

When she was fourteen, her family moved to San Jose, California. Seen as different, she was teased mercilessly by students at her high school. "They used to say horrible things to me—it was just embarrassing—and I hated to go to school," she told the San Jose Trans Oral History Project in 2019.

Around the same time, however, she discovered that St. James Park, site of a notorious lynching in 1933, was a popular gay cruising spot.

"I started going there. I met a whole bunch of kids....There was my best friend Bernie, Tommy, there was a whole list of them." There also was another attraction. "We used to, uh, prostitute. You know, the older men used to come and give us money for whatever they wanted us to do. That's how we got to be in a group." The men considered Elizondo to be "a really good looking boy at one time and I used to get a lot of money."

At age fifteen or sixteen, she began seeing an older man who one day took her to San Francisco, where they visited the Tenderloin. "I noticed that there was a lot of people like me," she later

After completing basic training in 1965, Felicia (then Felipe) Elizondo was stationed at the Coronado Naval Base before volunteering for service in Vietnam. *Felicia Elizondo Papers (2021-06), GLBT Historical Society.*

told Zachary Drucker of *Vice News*. "My God, it was the Mecca of gayness." Soon, she and Bernie would "play hooky from school and come into the Tenderloin on a Greyhound from San Jose," where "Compton's Cafeteria became "the center of the universe for us."

By the time she graduated high school, Elizondo had decided she did not want to be gay any longer. She and her friends "were lost souls trying to understand what future was in store for us." What she wanted instead was "to be normal," not yet understanding what normal was for her. She concluded that if it meant being "straight," military service would be her deliverance.

She tried to enlist in the army, but the army declined to accept her because, standing 5' 2", she did not meet its height requirements. She joined the navy instead. "If the navy didn't make me a man, nothing would," she decided. After completing basic training, Elizondo was stationed at the naval base in Coronado, California. "Then I decided that I wanted to volunteer for Vietnam because maybe I would get killed and maybe all this hurt and pain would go away."

She was in Vietnam about six months before the pressure of "passing for straight" became too much for her. "Being in Vietnam, being in Da

As an advocate for the transgender community, Elizondo remembered the Compton's Cafeteria Riot at an event commemorating its fiftieth anniversary, San Francisco, August 2016. *Photograph by Pax Ahimsa Gethen. Wikipedia.*

Nang and stuff like that, and seeing all those men! My god!" A charge that she was AWOL (with a French teacher) led her finally to tell the navy she was gay. She returned to the Bay Area with a dishonorable discharge, although she later successfully petitioned to have it changed to honorable.

The pieces of the puzzle of who she was came together while she was living in Chicago. "What changed my life was when I went to see the movie, *The Christine Jorgensen Story*," the so-called biography of the most famous transgender woman of her time, made by the gay director Irving Rapper, who also directed Bette Davis in five films. "I finally realized that this is who I am. I didn't know how I was going to get there, but where there is a will, there is a way."

Elizondo found a way. Moving back to San Jose, she eventually got a job with Pacific Bell as the first long-distance operator identified at birth as male in California history. In 1972, she began living full time as a woman. Two years later, when she completed her surgery, she finally was her true self. She was still working for the telephone company in 1987 when she was diagnosed with HIV.

After retiring, Elizondo moved to San Francisco "because the best possibility of surviving AIDS was the mecca of the medical center of everything." She became deeply involved with organizations that helped people living with HIV and AIDS, including the Shanti Project, Project Open Hand and PAWS. In addition, she estimated that she made some eighty panels for the AIDS Memorial Quilt.

Elizondo also became an advocate for the transgender community, especially trans women of color, who often were confronted with both racism and transphobia. Remembering the past was important to her, too, and she worked to keep alive the history of the Tenderloin as a haven, however tenuous it was, for trans people fifty years before. "Please don't forget all who came before you," she wrote in 2018, three years before she died. "You have to know where you have been to know where you are going."

ABOUT THE AUTHOR

Bill Lipsky received his doctorate in history from Carnegie Mellon University. He has been a visiting assistant professor of education at Pepperdine University, Los Angeles; a curriculum specialist with the Graduate School of Education, UCLA; and an instructional designer and program facilitator for Visa, Citicorp, MCI, Wells Fargo and the City and County of San Francisco, specializing in employee and management skills development. He is the author of *Gay and Lesbian San Francisco* (2006), a docent at the GLBT Museum and a member of the board of directors of the Rainbow Honor Walk. His monthly column, Faces from Our LGBT Past, appears in the *San Francisco Bay Times*.